Frankly Speaking

by

Frank Stapleton

BLACKWATER PRESS

Printed in Ireland at the press of the publishers 1991

© Blackwater Press 1991
8 Airton Road,
Tallaght,
Dublin 24.

ISBN 0 86121 313 0

Editor
Anna O'Donovan

Design & layout
Paula Byrne

Contents

Acknowledgements

I would like to thank the following people, without whose help this book would not have been possible: Victor & Hazel Wright, Arsenal Supporters Club, Cliff Butler, Manchester United Supporters Club and a special thanks to Paul Stretford for his input and tying up all the loose ends.

Frank Stapleton

Although every effort has been made to trace and contact some copyright holders of photographic material this has not always been possible. In such cases Blackwater Press will be happy to come to the normal arrangement should these copyright holders wish to contact us.

*This book is dedicated to
my wife Chris and my sons James and Scott*

A Domestic Career:

From Highbury to Ewood

Arsenal	*(1973-1980)*	**Manchester United**	*(1981-1988)*
Ajax	*(1988-1989)*	**Derby County**	*(1989)*
Le Havre	*(1989)*	**Blackburn Rovers**	*(1989-1991)*
(France)			

–1–
Early Arsenal Years

It was early July 1972, when I first set out on my career as a professional footballer. I had a trial some six weeks earlier, and the Chief Scout of the club, Mr Gordon Clark, had travelled to Dublin to meet my parents and discuss what my future would entail at a big city club like Arsenal. I remember at the time, my mother asking most of the questions and I don't think any of them were about football. She was, like any parent would be, concerned about where I would be living and what I would be doing when away from the football club. At the end of the meeting my mother was happy that I would be well looked after, so to the delight of myself and my father I signed apprentice professional forms with Arsenal.

My first day at the club was quite exciting, seeing all the first team players and having Liam Brady as a team-mate for the first time. After we were all introduced to each other, the manager Bertie Mee spoke and made it clear what was expected of us for the coming season. The team had just lost the Cup final to Leeds and had a good league position, so everyone was quite confident that the team could go one better the next time and win a trophy. Afterwards, it was off to the training ground in Hertfordshire where the work began in earnest.

My first job was to clean all the footballs in preparation for training that afternoon. So much for the glamour of professional football! When the public look at football they only see the finished article stepping out on a Saturday afternoon, but the real stars all begin by carrying out menial tasks, at clubs up and down the country. I think it is a very good system which helps to find out the character, commitment and passion of any young lad aspiring to be a star professional footballer – you learn the hard way, and those that finally make it to the top appreciate their position all the more.

During the following months a lot of changes occur in your life, both physically and mentally. Doing full-time training for the first time, feeling every ache and pain every time you move is something that your body and mind has to come to terms with. Also you have to contend with the mental pressure of being away from the care and protection of your parents and the ever-present feeling of home sickness. Arsenal have always had a good apprenticeship policy, letting the young players go home at regular intervals, thereby enabling the apprentices to settle quickly. The club has always had very high standards in terms of behaviour and dress, and these attributes were just as important in their eyes as the ability to play football.

In my first season of full-time football, I had a lot of ups and downs. I could play really well one week and the next have an absolute stinker, but this is all part of the learning process. Playing that first season for the youth team in the South East Counties League, I quickly noticed the players I played with and against were by far, more skilful than the players I had ever encountered before. The South-East counties League was very competitive and the standards high. I was made aware by the youth team coach, Ian Crawford, that I would have to work hard to improve my groundwork; I had always been good with my head but now I was competing with people who were as good as me in the air, but better with their feet, so I had a bit of work to do. Having said that, I scored thirty-six goals in my first season at the club, most of them with my head and had also struck up quite a good understanding with another young Irish man – Liam Brady. It was Liam's second season at the club – he had already played quite a few games in the reserves and was progressing very quickly. Nevertheless, I too was quite satisfied with my first year and was looking forward to the next.

About a month after my seventeenth birthday, I reached the first milestone of my intended career – signing professional forms for Arsenal. It was the next stage one reached after signing as an apprentice, more importantly, it meant I didn't have to do any more jobs around the ground. I had set myself a target for the forthcoming season, to break into the reserve team and hopefully gain a permanent place. However, things did not go like that at all – I was still scoring regularly but the coaches felt my ground work was still not good enough. Liam Brady was playing regularly in the reserves, also two other lads from Ireland had just signed apprenticeship forms, David O'Leary and John Murphy. I felt that things were progressing very slowly for me and I remember going to see the chief scout Gordon Clark on more than one occasion and discussing my situation with him. Gordon felt that I was letting mistakes affect me and that I needed to work harder. It was very difficult to hear and accept, other players who had come to the club at the same time were getting games in the second team whilst I was being overlooked. However, if anything, those meetings had made me even more determined to succeed and do whatever was necessary to get to the top.

Later in the season I received a letter from a club in S. Africa asking me if I would be interested in playing for them. I went to see the manager Bertie Mee and told him about the expressed interest. He said that S. Africa was a nice place and that if I wanted to go he would not stand in my way. I knew that if any club thinks you have got a future they would just dismiss things like that, but in this case I couldn't believe my ears, he was actually recommending it! Yet again, I would have to prove people wrong and decided I was too young to go to S. Africa and would stay on at the club.

Unfortunately it was a difficult time for me – I didn't get a reserve game until about six games from the end of the season. When I did get my chance my team-mates included Frank McLintock, Peter Marinello and Geoff Barnett. We were playing away at Cardiff and one thing that I remember, apart from scoring the only goal of the game, was the attitude of Frank McLintock. Here was a guy who had done everything in the game, captained the team to the double in 1971, encouraging young players to play, helping them with little tips and in general, leading by example. The easiest thing for him would have been to go through the motions on a soggy afternoon in Cardiff. After that game at Cardiff I played the remaining six games for the youth team and was beginning to show a better touch on the ground.

A couple of months before the season finished, the young professionals were all called into the coaches' room for a meeting. There was ten of us in all, five on one side and five on the other. After a general chat about how we felt we were doing, it was pointed out that in the opinion of the coaching staff, the five players on the right hand side of the room were the ones most likely to make the first team. The five players were Liam Brady, David Price, Richard Powling, Trevor Ross and Wilf Rostron. I just couldn't believe that they would make us feel so small by expressing such an opinion in public. I have always felt that if something has to be said, it should be said in private, on a one to one basis. Personally, I feel it was a big mistake because five people walked out of that room depressed and with very low self-esteem. I felt once again that I would have to prove people wrong.

Season of 1973/74

During the close season I worked very hard and was rewarded when I started off the new season in the reserves and more importantly, kept my place all season. The first team were struggling, going through a period of re-building. There were a lot of young players in the team mixed with players who had been on the double winning team of

1971. The likes of Alan Ball, George Armstrong, Peter Simpson, Pat Rice and Sammy Nelson were all experienced players, but even with all their experience it would still take time to blend the experience and youth together. But time is not what you always get at big clubs like Arsenal because they set such high standards. The supporters get restless and that can transmit itself onto the pitch and affect the confidence of the players, especially the younger ones.

As the season progressed towards Christmas, the team was not in a healthy position in the League, but with a long way to go and the F.A. Cup to come, it was still possible to salvage something from the season. The thing about playing for Arsenal is that you have to live with the pressure of reading in the papers every week about the players the clubs are going to sign. However, if you've got what it takes it does tend to motivate you and keep you on top of your game. The success of the first team tends to filter down to all levels of the club, because at the end of the day, it is the first team that brings the public into the ground. The first team did pick up in the second half of the season and just missed out on qualification for Europe. I had also established myself in the reserves but there still seemed little chance of a break-through to the first team with four players in front of me vying for two positions. The two players in possession were Brian Kidd and John Radford, with Charlie George and Brian Hornsby pushing for their places. By the end of the season, playing for the first team seemed as far away as ever.

Season 1974/75

At the start of every season each club in the league believes that they have what it takes to win the league. It's no different with players at whatever level they are playing – we all have hopes and ambitions for the coming seasons. The club had replaced Steve Burtenshaw with Bobby Campbell from QPR as first team coach. He had gained a good reputation and it was thought that he had what was necessary to change the fortunes of the club.

From our very first meeting, I took a dislike to Mr Campbell. He seemed to think that the reserves and youth team players were there to use and abuse. He could change in a second; for instance he could be talking to a first team player and, on seeing you appear around the corner, he would start shouting and antagonising, trying to making you look small. I think he came to Arsenal thinking that he could change things and run it the way he had done at QPR. That was probably his biggest mistake. The club had a lot of very good young players and instead of bringing them along by letting them develop in their own time as in previous years, he was pushing people too far and making a lot of enemies along the way. Bertie Mee was still the manager, but he just let Bobby Campbell do almost as he wanted – that in itself was another mistake. The team struggled for most of the season but I reached another personal milestone, making my debut on Easter Saturday 1975, against Stoke City at Highbury. We drew 1-1 but I struggled all afternoon and was eventually substituted after seventy minutes. I had mixed feelings that day – sad that I had not played too well but also happy that I had made my debut and and achieved a personal goal by playing in the first team.

Arsenal 1975/76

Season 1975/76 was the time when I really did make the big breakthrough. After the disappointment last season, not getting another game in the first team following my debut, I set my stall out to work very hard during the pre-season. I even got the bonus of been taken to a pre-season friendly against Hadjuk Split in Yugoslavia. It was a great experience and it gave me an insight into the type of unfriendly atmosphere you have to put up with when playing abroad.

There were rockets and bangers going off everywhere and the team we were playing were skilful but also very physical – and this was a friendly match! I think we played against teams like this because it improved our mental as well as physical strength. This was the type of cauldron you could expect when playing in the European competition.

Things had been going well during pre-season games, I had been scoring freely for the reserves, but I did not expect to be playing in the opening match for the first team. The manager usually started with the team that finished the previous season or new signings if he had made them in between. So, for the first game it was John Radford and Brian Kidd in the two front positions. I started the season with a reserve match away against Leyton Orient on the Wednesday. The first team had a game on the Tuesday. The reserve match ended 3-3 and although I didn't score, I felt that I had a good game.

Following the reserve match, I reported for training as usual on Friday and to my delight, found that I was in the squad for the match against Leicester City at Highbury the next day. John Radford was doubtful with a muscle strain and I was to play if he did not recover in time. As it transpired he didn't make it and I was in the starting line-up. On that day six Irishmen lined up for the Arsenal first team — Sammy Nelson, Pat Rice, Terry Mancini, David O'Leary, Liam Brady and myself. The game went well from a personal point of view. Liam sent over a great cross in the 15th minute and I headed us into the lead. On the day I could have had a hat-trick but their keeper, Mark Wallington, performed well and we conceded a late goal to get just a point. I was very pleased with my performance and it had all been televised.

Our next game was away in the League Cup against Everton on the following Tuesday. I was totally unprepared for what was about to happen – John Radford was fit again and Bertie Mee opted to bring him back into the team. I was extremely disappointed after everything that had happened, but the manager thought it necessary to use experienced players in a very difficult away match. The game did not go too well for us; we were 2-0 down mid-way through the second half and it looked like we were dead and buried. However, we pulled a goal back through Alex Cropley with twenty minutes to go, and ten minutes later I was brought on to try and improve the situation. With a minute to go, after a scramble in the goalmouth, I got the equaliser. If the manager thought he had a problem with selection for this match he had an even bigger selection headache after it.

I was picked for the next match but I knew that John Radford would not just sit back and accept it. He had been the perfect role model for me to watch. He would hold the ball up so well and his first touch was excellent, running off the ball to make space for team-mates. His strength and awareness around the penalty box made him a great all-round player. I knew I would have to play well in every match in order to keep my place and keep John Radford out.

From that point on I continued to hold my place right through the first half of the season but the results were not too good. The likes of Jimmy Rimmer, Alan Ball and Brian Kidd were playing very well, but again, with so many young players, inconsistency was the main problem. As the season progressed there was increasing pressure on the team especially after we were knocked out of the F.A. Cup in the 3rd round at Wolves. The manager decided he had to bring back the senior players to try to get the team out of trouble. I don't think that that was the only problem with the team – a lot of young players resented the coach, Bobby Campbell as he was constantly critical of them and never made remarks to the seniors. I think that he didn't want confrontation with the older players and always kept them happy but felt he could handle the youngsters in any way he chose.

As we neared the end of the season the team had picked up and climbed the table to safety. The club announced that Bertie Mee was to retire at the end of the season, though some believe that he had been asked to step down by the board.

There was a lot of speculation about who would take over. There were lads within the club who were convinced that Bobby Campbell would get the job. With this in mind, Alan Ball called a players' meeting and went round to each individual asking if he wanted Bobby Campbell to get the job. Most of the senior players voted for him but Liam Brady, Wilf Rostron and myself said no, that we would rather have somebody new. I could understand the older players' thinking. They reckoned that a new manager would make sweeping changes and most of them would be the first to go. Alan Ball also had a vested interest as he had been promised that if he had got the backing of the players he would get the coach's job. Alan went to the chairman with his findings and told him that the majority of the players would like Bobby Campbell to have the job. He was promptly told it was not a decision for the players but one which would be taken at boardroom level.

The last game of the season at Manchester City was a very emotional one. It was Bertie Mee's last game in charge. The players presented him with a momento, he was very overcome with emotion and left the room. Considering the success he had brought to the club, it was a very sad way for him to go. After that weekend Bobby Campbell was in charge until the official announcement of the new manager. It was during this period that Liam and myself were going back to Dublin for the summer. We were on our way out of Highbury for the airport, when Campbell asked us where we were going, we told him that we were on our way home, to Ireland. He became very hostile towards us and said that we had to be back at the end of the week to pick up the offers of new contracts. The next minute, Alan Ball walked through the door and ignored us and Bobby Campbell acted as if we did not even exist. We shrugged our shoulders and walked out of Highbury and headed for the airport.

The players were not the only ones Bobby Campbell had run-ins with. He had been giving the reserve and youth team coaches Ian Crawford and Roger Thompson a hard time since he had arrived at the club. He called them in for a meeting and said that since it looked certain that he was going to get the job he wouldn't have further use for them, as he was going to bring in his own people. He got a reply which he never expected as Ian Crawford exploded and said to him, "With all due respect to you Bobby, you haven't got the fucking job yet!"

At the end of the following week my offer arrived from the club by registered post. I was hoping that I would get a substantial pay rise considering that I had played twenty-five times for the first team and scored five goals in my first full season. When I opened the letter I got the biggest shock of my life, I had been offered £14-a- week pay rise for a three year contract with a further three year option. What the club in fact were hoping was that I would sign for six years for £70-a-week. The offer had been prepared by Bertie Mee as one of his last chores as manager. I couldn't believe it!

– 2 –
New Manager
1976/77

During the close season, the announcement came that Terry Neill had been appointed manager of Arsenal. It came as a shock for two reasons: one, he was the manager of Arsenal's biggest rivals Tottenham Hotspur and secondly it seemed that his job was secure and he was happy in it. During his time at Spurs he had been known to come out with some outrageous statements about his players in the press when they hadn't played so well, but the club were happy with the appointment particularly the Chairman, Denis Hillwood, who said that Terry had always belonged to Arsenal, and was now back where he belonged!!!

Terry Neill brought in his assistant from Spurs, Wilf Dixon and this left the current coaching staff not knowing what was going to happen to them. Usually a new manager is given a free hand to choose his backroom staff but the manager had other things to sort out before that. Brian Kidd had gone back North to play for Manchester City, so the manager had to replace him, and quickly. The signing of Malcolm MacDonald from Newcastle United for £333,333 was guaranteed a deal that would grab all the headlines – the fee was a record and the club was signing a proven goalscorer. It also helped to sell season tickets before the season started.

When Terry Neill decided to appoint his coaching staff there was a disappointment for Bobby Campbell. He was offered the job of reserve team coach, an offer which in itself was a slap in the face. He turned it down and left the club with bad feelings on both sides. The reserve and youth team coaches retained their jobs. The words of Ian Crawford must have been ringing loud and clear in Bobby Campbell's ears.

The job as Arsenal Manager is a difficult one at the best of times, but I don't think that Terry Neill could have foreseen the problems he would face when he took the job on. For a start he was still quite young (in those days clubs didn't have player managers) having only just stopped playing a couple of years earlier. He was coming to manage players that he had played with and therefore there was a bit of resentment. This situation reared its head when we went to Germany for a week of training. We had been training three times a day, every day, and when it came to Saturday, Terry decided that we were going to have a fourth session so the lads couldn't go to the local bar for a beer. The training session ended up as a nightmare because all the players took their frustrations out on each other and it was just a free for all. Two of the senior players, Alan Ball and Peter Storey did not even bother to turn up which made it even more of a farce. As far as I know nothing was ever said about it again.

Two weeks before the season started there was a tour to Switzerland and Yugoslavia, with three games to play. I knew that I would be playing as John Radford had to stay behind as one of his children was having an operation, so I thought there was a chance to form some sort of partnership with 'Supermac' as Malcolm MacDonald was known.

It was on this tour that I got a chance to speak to the new manager about my contract. I told him that in my opinion the terms were ridiculously low for a first team player. He replied that in his opinion they were very good and that there wouldn't be any increase as far as he was concerned. He added that I should sign the contract and not look for things which I didn't deserve. A £14-a-week increase for six years was hardly good by any standards but his response alerted me to the fact that Terry Neill did not have me in his plans for the future – this was well illustrated when we got back off the tour.

17

On the Wednesday before the season kicked-off, there was a practice match on the pitch and Supermac and John Radford were paired up front together. After training I went into see the manager and asked why I was not playing in the first team. His reply was that the team that had played that morning was the team for Saturday. I couldn't believe it – I thought he had been trying something different to see how it would work. I explained that Supermac and John had not kicked a ball together until then and I had played every game in pre-season with Supermac. I left his office telling him in no uncertain terms that his decision was a 'fucking joke', and slammed the door behind me.

The buildup for the match was as you would expect, big crowd, television cameras, new manager, new record signing and it was the newly promoted Bristol City's first game in the first division. I'm sure the manager must have had an inkling that it was not going to be his day when Liam Brady cried off with a flu bug on the morning of the game. The game turned out to be a nightmare for Arsenal and Terry Neill. The team generally didn't play well and Supermac and John Radford just didn't hit it off. It was neither player's fault – both were too set in their ways of playing and they didn't compliment each other at all. Also the team missed Liam Brady, he was generally at the centre of anything that was good about the our play. The game ended 1-0 to Bristol and they fully deserved it. As I sat in the stand watching, I couldn't help feeling a little bit smug and knew that the manager would find it uncomfortable in his aftermatch press conference.

At the next game against Norwich City on Wednesday, I was brought in to play with Supermac, and Liam returned after illness. The result was Arsenal 3, Norwich 1. Both Supermac and I scored, everyone was happy, and the performance was 100 per cent better than on Saturday. Supermac and myself blended quite well together as my strength of being able to win the ball in the air and Supermac's pace off the mark gelled well together. There had been speculation that weekend that Arsenal were about to transfer me to Luton in a part exchange deal plus £60,000. This was later confirmed to me by Malcolm MacDonald, who knew the Luton manager Harry Haslam from his time at the club. This confirmed my thinking – the manager wanted me out and was in the process of doing so behind the scenes.

After the Norwich match things just got better and better for me on the pitch. I had worked up a good understanding with Supermac, and I was getting my fair share of goals, but I was still only earning £56.00 a week and I was determined to get satisfaction one way or another.

About a month into the season I told Terry Neill that I needed to speak to him again concerning my contract. He said, "There is nothing to talk about, the terms remain the same," and he walked away. Right there and then I decided to take things into my own hands. I spoke to a reporter who worked for the *People* newspaper and told him that I would be seeking a meeting with Terry Neill that week and that he would have to give me a pay rise or a transfer.

When I arrived for training on Monday morning the manager called me into his office and said he couldn't believe that I had spoken to such a reporter. He said that I was not getting a pay rise, I did not deserve one and told me to get out of the office.

After that I was more determined than ever to be satisfied. A couple of nights later I went to see the Chief Scout, Gordon Clark (who had brought me over from Dublin). I let him know what had happened and told him that I wished to put in a written transfer request. He helped me to write it and put the appropriate words in the right places. He also told me that there was a board meeting the next morning and that I should hand the letter to the secretary for the Chairman, when he arrived at 8.30 am. The following morning I handed the secretary, Ken Friar, the envelope he said to me, "Is that what I think it is?" I told him that it was, and he replied, "Not another one! Can we discuss it?" I refused, and walked out.

The response was the most amazing turnaround I have ever experienced. The next morning as soon as I arrived, I was summoned to see the manager. He asked me why I had not spoken to him about my feelings before taking this action and said that the Chairman had torn the letter up and flatly refused to grant the request. Continuing on, he said that he wanted to give me a rise and that I deserved it, but because of government restrictions at the time, he could not. A different tune to five days before! I could not accept what he was saying and said that the Chairman might have to tear up a few more requests before I was finished. A few weeks later I played my first game for the Republic of Ireland against Turkey in Aukara. When I returned due to my new status as an 'international player', I was offered signed a new contract and finally got my long awaited pay rise.

Even though I had secured a new contract, I knew I couldn't rest on my laurels. The club was still on the lookout for players and I knew that if I did not maintain my form I would be out of the team. The team was playing quite well but the big problem was Supermac – he was not hitting the net as often as he had at his other clubs. I think the problem was his adjustment to Arsenal's style of play. When he was at Newcastle all the play was directed at Supermac getting the ball over the top of the defence. The Arsenal style was to play the ball to feet and probe for openings. Also, as with all players he needed a settling in period, but unfortunately he did not get that because of the amount paid for him. All the lads were confident and knew that it would work out for him sooner rather than later.

The team now had a good blend of youth and experience. Players like Trevor Ross, David O'Leary, Liam Brady and myself were complimented by Alan Ball, George Armstrong, Pat Rice and Peter Storey. Pat Howard had been bought from Newcastle to play alongside O'Leary. Our home form had been excellent, unbeaten since the first game of the season. We had reached the quarter final of the league Cup only to lose 2-1 to QPR after leading 1-0 and missing a penalty. We were always in the top six of the league but I still felt we did not have the strength in the squad to actually catch up the leaders – Liverpool, Ipswich and Aston Villa. Our away form was very patchy and after a couple of defeats the manager had criticised us publicly in the papers just as he had done when he was at White Hart Lane. Personally, I don't think this helped the situation. Players can accept criticism in the dressing room as long as it stays there. The worst thing for any professional player, is to read in the paper the next morning what had been said after the match in the privacy of the dressing room.

A big shock for most of the supporters was the departure of Alan Ball to Southampton. In the dressing room it just seemed a matter of time before Alan would leave, after he had clashed with Terry Neill during one of our team meetings. Terry had been talking about some of our players not looking interested in games. Alan said that it stemmed from training which he felt was repetitive and boring. From that day on, Alan Ball's days as an Arsenal player were numbered. Also, on that day John Radford was transferred to West Ham for £80,000. I suppose I should have felt that was one less player to challenge for my place, but we were letting a very good player go, and there was no immediate replacement available.

Alan Hudson was signed by Terry Neill to replace Alan Ball, so it took a bit of the disappointment away for the supporters with the signing of another English international midfielder.

After the turn of the year our form dipped. Again it was our away form which was letting us down so we had to hope for a good Cup run. We beat Coventry 3-1 in the third round, but then drew Jack Charlton's Middlesborough away, a bit of a bogey side especially at Ayresom Park. We lost the tie 3-0 and it more or less ended our season. The best we could hope for was a high position to qualify for Europe. We did not make that either, and I also felt that there was still a little bit of uneasiness beneath the surface. The criticism was still appearing in the paper after matches and the players were getting fed up with being criticised publicly. It had even been hinted that the Chairman had had a word with the manager and said that it wasn't the way an Arsenal manager should conduct himself. Nevertheless, it was not going to be forgotten quickly and would rear it's ugly head again in the near future.

– 3 –
Season 1977/78

When we reported back for pre-season training in early July we were told that there was a tour planned to Singapore and Australia. Also on the tour were Glasgow Celtic, managed by Jock Stein, and Red Star Belgrade. It seemed a strange choice because it involved a lot of travelling and with kick-off for the new season just over a month away, it was going to be tiresome for the players. There had been a lot of rumblings in the dressing room and it had originated from most of the older players. Alan Hudson had not hit it off with Terry Neill, and Malcolm MacDonald had words with him on more than one occasion. We were still without a first team coach, and Liam Brady had also commented to Terry Neill a couple of times the previous season that the training had become boring and repetitive.

After five days hard training we set off on the fifteen-hour plane journey to Singapore. We played our first game against Red Star and lost 3-1 after extra time but played really well on the night. Our next game was against the Singapore National team, who had lost to Celtic. We won 5-1 but it could not have been seen as a stern test. After the game Terry announced that Dave Sexton was joining as first team coach and would be meeting us in Australia. However, Terry's plans were in ruins the very next day when Dave Sexton was announced as Manchester United's new manager.

There had been an undercurrent all through the trip and it all came to a head when we arrived in Sydney to play our first match. We arrived about breakfast-time and immediately went for something to eat. Most of the players were half-way through their meal when

Malcolm started shouting and screaming, saying that he had been given a child's bed and that it was not good enough. Most of the lads couldn't keep their faces straight, because he sounded like a spoilt kid who had not got his own way.

The fiasco continued – a couple of days later we lost to the national team and the morale of the players was very low. When we arrived in Adelaide, everything went out of control. After lunch, it was standard practice that most of the players went to rest for the afternoon before training in the evening, but Hudson and MacDonald decided to have a chat and a drink with the Chairman Denis Hill-Wood. They were still with the chairman when Terry came over and told them to get to bed and rest. A few minutes later Terry came back and told both Alan Hudson and SuperMac that they were going to return to England on the next available plane. Both players went to bed and got a flight out that evening. The rest of us were told of the situation, but it didn't surprise me as it had been bubbling under the surface for a long time.

The situation continued from bad to worse, it did not take long to reach the press and soon there was an army of photographers parked outside the hotel. The whole situation was handled very badly. Terry could easily have left the players out of the match and dealt with the situation when we got back to England but instead his actions meant that the club's name was dragged through the mud and the whole affair got out of hand. The three people involved all sold their stories to Sunday Papers but the Chairman stepped in, told them to sort it out and that he did not want to read about it anymore. After all that had happened it was a relief to get the season started and do what we all wanted to do – play football. Both players were on the transfer list but Hudson went a step further and vowed he would never play for Arsenal again.

There had been no major signings in pre-season, so we were lining up almost the same as the season before, but this also meant that if a crop of injuries came all at once we would be struggling to make a challenge for the title. We made a mediocre start to the season but Terry made a signing which I think was the best decision he ever made and it did not involve a player – Don Howe came in as first team coach. He changed the training routines, worked us hard and demanded more from the players both on and off the pitch. He was the perfect foil for Terry, because Don took all the training sessions which allowed the manager to take more of a back seat in the day to day training of the team. In my opinion, Don was an exceptional coach, he could pin-point what was going wrong in a second and constantly worked with the players to improve their game.

It was not long before Don's influence was showing on the park. He got Alan Hudson playing again and was influential in bringing Alan Sunderland to Highbury just after Trevor Ross had left to join Everton. We were more organised and with Liam Brady and Alan Hudson in midfield there was plenty of flair in the team. We were always short of a championship winning squad but we were definitely a good bet in the Cup competitions.

We stayed in the top five all season but never really got close to Nottingham Forest who were going really strong.

The F.A. Cup had always meant a lot to Arsenal and it generated a lot of excitement amongst the supporters in the years gone by.

But when we were drawn away to Sheffield Utd in the third round it looked like a very tough draw. We went to Yorkshire and beat them 5-0, a tremendous result especially when most people were expecting a shock result. Our results had picked up in the league and we were playing with a lot more consistency and a settled team. We beat Wolves and Walsall to reach the quarter finals of the Cup and reached the semi-final of the League Cup where we lost over two legs to Liverpool even though we felt we were the better side over the two games. It seemed to give the team more resolve and it is the only semi-final in which I have been on a losing side.

As the season wore on, it seemed that the Cup was going to be our best bet for a trophy. We had been drawing too many games in the league but when the Cup came round we seemed to relish the situation and came out on top. We beat Wrexham 3-2 away to reach the semi-finals where we were drawn against Orient who were in the Second Division so we were favourites to go through to the final. We beat Orient 3-0 and Malcolm claimed two goals, which were both own goals but it looked good on his statistics at the end of the season. The man of the match that day was Graham Rix who scored the other goal and was putting Alan Hudson under extreme pressure for his place. There were great celebrations afterwards as we had reached the final where we were playing Ipswich, who had beaten West Brom in the other semi-final.

The week of the final was all razzmatazz with the press having time to spend with the players early in the week. They were all looking for different angles to use on the day of the match but one *Sun* newspaper photographer went a little bit too far. He asked the six Irishmen on the team if they would come onto the pitch and do a picture with an Irish angle. When we got there he had picks and shovels ready for us to pose with. Needless to say, it did not go down too well. However, a compromise was reached when we agreed to pose with dummy rifles and helmets.

The manager and Don, kept our training routine the same and we only went into a hotel on the Friday afternoon. No one knew what the team was likely to be because there was a big doubt about Liam's ankle and he had been struggling for weeks to get it right. Terry had left it up to Liam himself to decide whether he was fit or not, knowing that he would do the right thing. But Terry had another decision to make – whether to stick with Alan Hudson or play Graham Rix who had been the star of the semi-final. Normally Terry would have gone with experience but Hudson had turned up late for training on Monday, half-cut, and got a right ear-bashing from Don

Howe who reminded him that the most important game of his life was coming up in five days time. In the end, Hudson was picked and Graham Rix was very disappointed. His chance, however, would come again.

The final itself was a blur – it just passed us by. Ipswich fully deserved their win, they were hungry for the ball and wanted to win more than us. If it had not been for Pat Jennings it could have been a very embarrassing scoreline. Before we knew it, we were back in the dressing room, a defeated team who had played to only 50 per cent of our capability. Liam had limped off in the second half but we were second best all afternoon, in every department. I was extremely disappointed.

On the following Monday we had a meeting to try and work out why we had played so poorly. Don Howe criticised Malcolm MacDonald heavily and suggested to him that he had gone out to play for himself. Malcolm, to his credit, was very honest and agreed that all he wanted to do was to score a goal at Wembley in a Cup Final regardless of the result. Liam Brady admitted that he should not have played but did because he thought that the chance to play in a Cup Final might not come along again. We all knew that we did not do ourselves justice but resolved that we would go back the following season and win it. I suppose every losing team says that but the players knew they had to put the record straight.

– 4 –

Arsenal 1978/79
The Maturing Year

After the pre-season break everyone had got the disappointment of the Cup Final out of their system and were looking forward to the new season with renewed confidence. Terry Neill had bought Paul Barron as understudy to Pat Jennings for £70,000 and sold John Matthews to Sheffield Utd for £90,000, but with money in the bank from the F.A. Cup he was still looking to strengthen the squad further.

After going through four weeks of Don Howe's crippling pre-season training the lads were delighted to have in their sights the first Saturday of the season. We were at home to Leeds United and 42,000 people turned up to watch. It ended 2-2, but Liam was absolutely magnificent scoring two goals, and his performance was world class. As we progressed into the season it was apparent that Liam was showing the ability and maturity that everyone knew he possessed, but there are times when even a genius can be frustrated and it ended up with him and Don Howe having a right go at each other.

We played Rotherham in a second round league Cup tie and were expected to win comfortably. We took an early lead but, from that moment on, our performance got steadily worse. Mid-way through the second half Malcolm MacDonald went down injured as his knee had locked. Fred Street, our Physio. managed to unlock it and Malcolm came back on. He had only been on a minute when it locked again and eventually he was taken off. We were 3-1 down and never looked like getting back in the game and at the end Don Howe went potty about the performance. Liam reacted by saying that we had been playing with ten men because there was no way Malcolm could have been fully fit. We had not started the league off too well and this defeat to a third division team had not helped matters.

Some of the supporters even stayed behind to ask Terry Neill what the hell was going on. I think that Liam Brady was not the only one frustrated on the night. Having done so well in the Cup competitions the previous season this result was a disaster for us and indicated that the previous season had been a flash in the pan. The team then showed true grit and starting with a 5-1 thrashing of QPR on the following Saturday, we only lost two games out of the remaining seventeen. Don's way was always to get things out in the open, with every player being given the opportunity to contribute and air their views. On more than one occasion it had helped to clear the air after a bad defeat or a run of games where we had not played too well.

The best win of the run came on Boxing Day, when we travelled to play arch rivals, Tottenham Hotspur at White Hart Lane and beat them 5-0 with over 42,000 fans watching. By the end of the game there were only Arsenal supporters in the ground as the Spurs supporters were so disgusted with their team that they had left. Alan Sunderland scored a hat trick that day and it only confirmed what a good player he was. Alan had switched into the middle to play alongside me after Malcolm had gone into hospital with his knee problem. We hit it off straight away – Alan was very quick off the mark and he would pick up 90 per cent of my flick-ons. The partnership just seemed to happen without either of us having to think about it. The best thing about the partnership was that we were scoring goals regularly and working hard for each other. Whenever one of us had an off day the other would work that little bit harder to make up for it. He was easily the best partner that I ever played with.

We also became firm friends off the field which helped to make our partnership even stronger. I think it helped having Liam Brady playing the best football of his career, and also Graham Rix had established himself, once Alan Hudson left to join Seattle Sounders earlier in the season. The whole team seemed to be perfectly balanced with Pat Jennings playing better than ever and David O'Leary and Willie Young as good as any central defenders in the country. The only problem was that if we got any injuries or sudden loss of form, we did not have the strength in the reserves. We had Steve Walford, Steve Gatting and Jimmy Harvey but the rest of the youngsters had no experience and were not ready yet.

Playing in Europe is special for any footballer, gathering your wits against teams who play a different style and who sometimes can play like robots to achieve a result. Nevertheless, the English game is well respected in Europe and teams know they are going to have a tough game if they draw an English team. In the first round we drew an East German team, Locomotive Leipzig, playing the first leg at home. We struggled, mainly trying to break down their defence but we got the breakthrough with twenty minutes to go and ended up winning 3-0, with Alan Sunderland and myself both scoring goals. They had frustrated us for most of the match but we had learned an invaluable lesson – to be patient and chances would come.

The away leg was a formality and we romped home 4-1. I scored an unusual hat trick, two for Arsenal and one for Locomotive. Needless to say they did not get the honourary hat-trick ball.

The next round was tougher drawing Hadjuk Split of Yugoslavia who were seasoned campaigners in Europe. It was back to the place where I had gone on my initial trip with the first team and the atmosphere was definitely more electric than the previous occasion. We came away with a respectable 2-1 defeat in what turned out to be a very physical match. We had got the precious away goal and needed to win only 1-0, to go through. The game was everything that was bad about European football, spitting, kicking, niggling tackles and incidents off the ball. It all got too heated and Liam Brady was sent off for retaliation after his marker had fouled him, yet again, and the frustration of us not getting the goal we needed finally got to him. To our relief, in the very last minute Willie Young headed in the winner and we were through, but Liam Brady was banned and could not play in the next round. The lads hoping we would draw a big name team and not a drab Eastern European club.

It was not to be, we drew Red Star Belgrade who had beaten West Brom in the previous round with a last minute goal. The first leg was away and we felt satisfied with just one goal to pull back when we got back to Highbury. It was a cold December night when we played Red Star. They had shown that they had some good players during our first leg, and they came determined to hold onto what they already had. We scored the goal we needed through Alan Sunderland midway through the second half and we were pushing for the winner when Mark Heeley who had replaced Liam was injured. Whilst he was receiving attention and we were trying to get our substitute on, they broke away and got an equaliser. At that moment it was all over, they shut up shop and we were out of Europe. It was a painful lesson, inside a minute we had lost a tie we had looked set to win.

It was coming up to Christmas and I had just been awarded supporters' "Player of the year". They vote from January to December and it was a great honour considering how well Liam Brady had been playing since the start of the season. The F.A. Cup had come round again and memories of Ipswich returned, though we had gained some revenge by beating them 4-1 in the league in November, when I scored my first hat trick for the club, this time I got the ball. We had a tricky game away to third division Sheffield Wednesday, who were managed by Jack Charlton whose teams were always tough and dour rather than being attacking and exciting.

We played at Hillsborough and got a 1-1 draw on an icy pitch. As Pat Jennings came out for the second half he was pelted with snowballs and the game could not restart because he could not get to his goal. We thought we had done the hard part but we had not

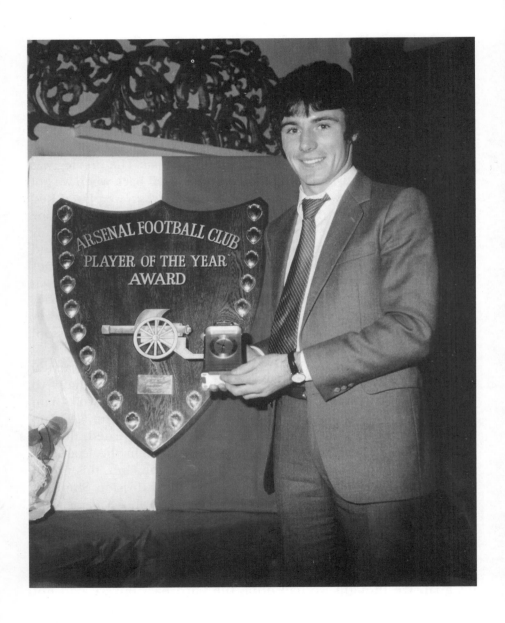

reckoned on the fighting qualities of Jack's team. They came to Highbury and took a shock lead midway through the first half. It looked like we were going out of the Cup, it was one minute to ten past nine on the famous Highbury clock, only six minutes left, when Alan Sunderland sent over a far post cross, I headed it down to Liam Brady who poked it into the top corner. The sighs of relief could be heard all over the ground. Extra time couldn't sort it out either and it was on to Leicester for a second replay.

The game went from end to end but despite goals from both sides there was no outcome. It ended 2-2, and we went back to Leicester to play again two days later. This turned out to be even more exciting and produced two goals more than the previous game, a 3-3 draw. It was getting as long as the Forsythe saga. We had to go back to Leicester again the following Monday night. With the next round approaching, the F.A. were getting a little worried that the tie would never end. We had to work hard to get a 2-0 win, with Pat Jennings making two great saves near the end to deny them a score. It was all over after five games and we had only got into the fourth round!

We beat Notts County 2-0 in the fourth round and then drew Notts Forest, the reigning league champions away in the fifth round. Forest had not lost once at home in fifty matches and it was the hardest draw anyone could get.

From the kick-off we pinned back in our own half and Forest missed two good chances to go ahead, but the spirit and determination of the team kept us going throughout the game. In one real attack of the game we got a free kick, Liam Brady floated over a cross and I headed past Shilton. It was completely against the run of play and we had to battle until the final whistle to reach the draw for the quarter finals. During this period our league form had been erratic and it was inevitable that we would lose some games. However, Don Howe insisted that we could not turn form on and off like a tap and kept at us to keep the momentum going in all games.

We had added Brian Talbot to the squad and he had fitted in immediately, contrasting his strength and stamina with Liam and Graham's silky skills. I was having my best scoring spell to date for the club with twenty-one goals in all competitions. Looking back I think this was due to the other players around me playing well and creating the chances.

With our League form dipping, Terry and Don were getting increasingly worried that we were depending on our Cup run to achieve success, so we had another of those clear the air open talks the day after losing 2-0 to Ipswich, and the day before we played Southampton in the Cup. Whether the discussions would work this time they didn't know until the end of the game. We went a goal down early on and instead of everyone's head dropping it made us lift our game and play true to our real form. Southampton were formidable opposition at home but David Price one of our unsung heroes scored the equaliser to bring it back to Highbury two days later. It was probably the most important goal David ever scored in his life for Arsenal.

In the replay Alan Sunderland scored two superb goals to put us through to the semi-final for the second year in a row. There were only ten days to go before the semi-final and Wembley was again on the lips of everyone connected with the club.

Prior to the semi-finals, there was a a tremendous boost for the players and the club, Liam Brady was named "Player of the year", by his fellow professionals, the highest honour any player can achieve. He had been the model of consistency all season, with only the one blemish against Hadjuk Split. It had been nice to see one of our team-mates get the recognition he thoroughly deserved. What made the award so important for the team was that the recognition was rubbing off on everybody else.

Our chances of winning the League got smaller and smaller as we progressed further in the Cup – again it was down to the depth of our squad. There could be no other real excuse because Liverpool had also reached the semi-finals of the Cup and were still top of the League. They had a stronger squad and their reserves were established first team players, somehow Liverpool managed to keep them all happy. As our position in the League worsened it became increasingly important for us to win the Cup in order to qualify for Europe, but there was still Wolves to overcome before we could once again travel down Wembley way.

Just like the previous year's final, the week before the game Liam Brady was doubtful, this time with a knee injury and it would not be decided until they day of the game whether he would play or not. Again the decision would be left up to him. On the morning of the game Liam decided against playing saying he had made a mistake the year before and would not jeopardise our chances by playing when not 100 per cent fit.

We were staying at the Holiday Inn in Birmingham, which was next to Central TV studios. A friend of Terry's, the comedian Frank Carson, was working there and was invited to come and have lunch with us. I think Terry Neill saw it as a way of easing the tension but Frank never stopped talking. Nobody could get a word in edgeways and he ended up staying to watch the mid-day football magazine programme with us. All the lads liked to watch it, and usually there was deadly silence in the room but Frank kept telling the same jokes all the time and in the end Terry asked Frank to leave as we were about to start our team talk session. He had certainly taken our minds off the game!

The game was, as are all semi-finals, tense and tight. No side was willing to take any chances and it resulted in both defences dominating. However, I did feel good on the day and it was a day when there was not going to be many chances about. We went in 0-0 at half time and it might not have been a bad idea to have brought Frank Carson on – at least to keep everyone awake. But semi-finals are about results and not performances and such was the spirit in our team that we were not going to be denied. Terry and Don told us that the game was there for the taking but that if we were to settle for a draw, we could end up losing it. We stepped up the tempo in the second half and were pressing for a breakthrough.

David Price poked a ball through to me on the edge of the box. I turned and managed to hit it in my stride and before I knew it the ball was in the net and the Arsenal end of the ground was ecstatic. A little later Alan Sunderland scored a second and we were on our way to Wembley again. It was to be against the country's other glamour team Manchester United, though we did not know immediately because United needed two games to dispose of Liverpool.

It was named the glamour Cup final, Arsenal v Manchester United, two of England's greatest clubs. Maybe for the supporters, but for the club and players it was qualification into Europe and as neither had qualified through league position it became twice as important for both clubs to win. We had played nine games since the semi-final and had only won two, so it was a bit worrying for Terry and Don. What maybe helped us not to feel too bad, was the fact that Manchester United were going through the same sort of run.

Our preparation for the game was completely different to the previous year. We went to Bisham Abbey, a training centre for the England international team to use, and trained for two full days. It was like pre-season all over again.

Don Howe was leaving nothing to chance, making sure we were finely tuned for Saturday. That year there was no firm favourite and it took the pressure off us a little, but it is all about who performs on the day – League form has nothing to do with it.

– 5 –

The Cup Final

We had no injury problems and the team picked itself. Supermac had got himself fit but was not considered because he had not played enough games over the season to justify a place in the team, though he himself had always thought he had a chance until the team was announced.

What a great sporting occasion the F.A. Cup final is, and on 12 May 1979 it was scorching hot. It was going to be physically as well as mentally difficult, but we had gone through it last year and were determined to make it our day. We had powered into a 2-0 lead but the game was not a classic, United were not playing as well as they could have. It was 2-0 at half time, but the next goal was going to determine where the Cup was going. The game had gone into the last five minutes when Gordon McQueen pulled one back, but as far as we were concerned it was only a consolation. Then the unbelievable happened, Sammy McIlroy weaved his way past three defenders and poked the ball past Pat Jennings. They had equalised with two minutes to go! I remember thinking, "Oh no, we've blown it, we're fated not to win anything". From the kick-off Liam Brady picked the ball up and carried it forward, laid it off to Graham Rix who crossed and there was Alan Sunderland to sidefoot it home at the far post. In one minute I had gone from the depths of despair to the heights of ecstasy. The last minute seemed to last a lifetime but when the final whistle blew, the highs and lows of the season seemed to fade into oblivion. The last five minutes of the match would go down in history and people would say that it was one of the greatest Cup finals ever, but until that last five minutes I think that it was one of the most unspectacular games at Wembley had seen.

It was a great feeling having finally won something, probably the most satisfying because it was the first one and there was no guarantee of ever winning anything else. However, there was something now to fight for – an attempt to win the League championship. If we could keep all our players and bring in one or two more there was a real possibility

In training

– 6 –
Arsenal 1979/80

After the Cup final there had been a lot of speculation that Liam Brady, David O'Leary and myself would be leaving the club. The Chairman had said that if foreign clubs tried to sign us then Arsenal could not compete with them. My contract, and David's were up and Liam Brady had a year to run on his. We both signed new two-year contracts but Liam Brady could not agree a new one with Terry Neill and so remained on the terms of his present contract of the time. I thought the club could have shown good faith by giving Liam a pay rise, particularly for the way he had performed throughout the last season, but they wouldn't do it without him extending his contract.

The first match of the new season was at Wembley against Liverpool, the league champions in the Charity Shield. This game would tell us how far we had come and what would be needed to win the league. On the day we failed miserably, completely outplayed by a Liverpool team in which Dalgliesh scored two goals in a 3-1 win. On the Monday morning after the game, we spent three hours with Don Howe and Terry Neill discussing the reasons why we had played so badly and how we could bridge the gap between the two teams. We had only signed John Hollins from QPR so it was almost the same squad as last season. I felt it was now the time to sign two top class players to make the squad more competitive. We had lost Malcolm MacDonald, he had to retire because of injury, so there was no cover for Alan or myself. Maybe the players were not available or the club were reluctant to go into the red but it was obvious that we needed something to maintain a challenge.

It took us a while to get going in the League. Of the first ten games we had only won three, but the best was yet to come in the League Cup when we scored seven at Highbury in the second leg of the second round. The plus side was that three young players, Devine, McDermott and Vaessen had staked claims for places in the first team. In the European Cup Winners Cup we had beaten Fernebashe of Turkey 2-0 at Highbury and were preparing for a hot reception when we went to Istanbul. There was an intimidating atmosphere in the country because of martial law and the hotel was surrounded by troops. The stadium was full and they even had a guy who went around the stadium with a drum whipping the supporters up into a frenzy. We kept our heads and left the stadium with probably what in hindsight was the best result for everybody, a 0-0 draw.

The exploits of the previous season had created a great togetherness in the dressing room. Football is a team game and anything that is achieved is always done so as a unit, but in every dressing room you need somebody who is going to make you laugh – a character – we had two in Sammy Nelson and Willie Young. No one was immune to Sammy's wicked tongue. If someone came into training wearing something a little bit bright or a mixture of colours they were tormented all through training and dared to wear it again! The very next time they wore it they would go through the same ritual. Sammy was a great one for practical jokes. He once put Algipan, which is used for getting your muscles warm in the winter, into Graham Rix's underpants. That afternoon after training Graham was driving home when he experienced this terrible hot burning sensation. He had to grin and bear it until he arrived home and rip the offending items off. But Sammy was a great professional and was one of the hardest players I have ever known – he would kick his grandmother if he had to!

Willie Young was a big rugged Scotsman who complemented David O'Leary perfectly. He would put his head in anywhere and scored a lot of important goals for us. He was different to Sammy in that Terry Neill used to always be at the butt of his jokes. Willie would always have a moan about anything that we had to do, and if Terry announced something Willie would would moan even if he agreed with it! He had that sort of relationship with Terry who understood when he was being serious or not, otherwise he would never have got away with half of the things he used to say.

As we continued in the League our form at home was very worrying. We were drawing too many games but our away form was keeping our position in the league. Up until the end of the year we had only lost two league games away from home. We were knocked out in the semi-final of the league Cup by Swindon over two legs, after earlier in the competition knocking out Southampton and Brighton. We had reached in the quarter-finals of the European Cup Winners Cup and the F.A. Cup had not yet started for us. We were in fourth position at the turn of the year and still in two Cups but we had signed no one since July. There was also the prospect of losing Liam who had announced that he was leaving at the end of the season. It put an enormous amount of pressure on him, though he was playing well. When he had an off day sections of the crowd were quick to get on his back which was very unfair, considering the service he had given.

Again, as in previous seasons the Cup competitions started to take over our season. In the F.A. Cup, Cardiff were knocked out in the third round after a replay. Our league form was maintained with four successive wins against Derby, Aston Villa, Bolton and Stoke. With the games coming fast and furious, Terry and Don decided to rest players so they didn't burn themselves out before the end of the season. It was then that our league results began to falter, never was a strong squad needed more than now. We went through to the sixth round of the Cup by beating Brighton and Bolton respectively.

We then had two quarter-finals within four days of each other. The first was against Gothenburg in the European Cup Winners Cup and we booked our passage to the semi-finals with a 5-1 first leg win. The second was the F.A. Cup against Watford who had been the giant killers of the Cup that year, and it was going to be as tough as it could get. I got the two goals that day, that put us through to our third semi-final in successive years but Watford pulled a goal back near the end and made us really work for the win. In the return leg in Gothenburg we got a 0-0 draw to go comfortably through to the semi-finals.

In the semi-finals of the F.A. Cup we were drawn against Liverpool, with Everton playing West Ham in the other. The headlines in the papers were all about a Merseyside final, which suited us fine because it put the pressure firmly on their shoulders. In the European Cup Winners Cup we were drawn against Juventus, the top Italian team – we knew then that we would have to beat the top two teams in Europe to reach both finals.

As it always seems to turn out, the two games were in the same week. The Juventus game was first and I have never seen so many people packed into Highbury – 52,000 fans created a wonderful atmosphere.

It seemed that every Italian Restauranteur in London was there. The game was very eventful with Juventus scoring from the penalty spot after Bettega had been fouled. The stadium erupted when Bettega went over the top of the ball and went down David O'Leary's shin. It was so blatant I don't know how he stayed on the pitch but he got away with a yellow card. David was replaced by Pat Rice and we very quickly got back into our stride. It seemed to have shaken the Italians more than us, but they are masters of defence and later in the game when Tardelli was sent off for an ordinary foul on Liam, they still looked like holding on. In the very last minute we got the equaliser when Bettega put through his own net – who said there's no justice! – but it meant that we had to win in Turin to qualify for the finals.

We had only played Liverpool once since the Charity Shield and that had been a 0-0 draw at Highbury. All the press build up had been about that game and we were not expected to be able to hold them. As it happened the game turned out to be a huge disappointment, the only chance with five minutes to go, falling to Brian Talbot but his lobbed shot landed on top of the bar and bounced over. So it was a replay at Villa Park that both teams had to face the following Wednesday. The game was fought tooth and nail and at the end of it all, another draw. This time 1-1. The replay had to wait for twelve days because we had a league game against Liverpool and then the second leg in Turin.

There was very little time to think, just rest in between games. We needed very little training because the League games were piling up due to all the Cup commitments. But ask any player and he will tell you that being involved is still the best thing.

The league game with Liverpool was another draw but our minds were clearly on Juventus. The controversy over the David O'Leary/Bettega incident was still going on. Bettega had a TV show in Italy and he wanted David to go on it, but David declined as it would have been used for Bettega's benefit. The way the game went said a lot about the Italian temperament, they sat back and were happy to soak the pressure up and catch us on the break. With twenty minutes to go Paul Vaessen and John Hollins came on for David Price and Brian Talbot. It didn't matter now whether we lost by an away goal or five clear goals. With two minutes to go Graham Rix put over a beautiful cross and Paul Vaessen headed it in. The Italians were in disarray and did not know what to do, but there was no time for them to score – we had done the impossible – and the scenes at the end of the game in the dressing room will always live with me.

We continued the celebrations back at the hotel in Asti and at about five in the morning John Hollins and Alan Sunderland were going around the hotel on this child's motorbike, singing and waking everyone up! The adrenalin was still flowing which really made it difficult to sleep. We had reached one final but had won nothing yet.

The next Liverpool game turned out to be the best match so far. Alan scored after fifteen seconds and then Pat Jennings made some wonder saves to keep us in the game. Thoughts of Wembley came flooding back and we had to endure thirty more minutes in which Pat Jennings single-handedly kept us in it. Yet another replay, this time at Coventry, but it was only ten days before the final. Brian Talbot scored after twelve minutes and this time we held on to reach our third final in a row.

It seemed like we had been playing for twelve months solid because of the number of games we had played. Don Howe banned all talk of being tired and there was no time to think about anything as the next game was already on top of us. We had two league games before the F.A. Cup final, and once the second of those was over, it was a matter of concentrating on Wembley. There was no big build up like in previous years due to the lack of time. It was such a momentous effort against Liverpool that the final seemed like a little bit of an anti-climax. The opposition were West Ham, who were in the second division and who were not supposed to provide too stiff a test. We had learned not to under-estimate anybody and that things don't always happen as the so called "experts" would have us believe.

The final is a motivation in itself and playing at Wembley makes that feeling even stronger, but no players knows how he is going to play until the game starts and you hope that the mental strain has not taken too much out of you. On the day we couldn't raise a gallop, though West Ham played well. They only played one player in the middle up front and crowded the midfield to stifle our short passing game. In the end they deserved it but we had played well below par. The Liverpool saga had caught up with us.

The game in Brussels against Valencia in the final of the Cup Winners Cup was our sixty-eighth game of the season. Terry and Don had given us a good team talk before the game, and pointed out that we needed to lift our game if we hoped to win. The Spaniards had two world renowned stars in Mario Kempes and Rainer Bonhof, but we had a better all-round team and we felt that if we kept Kempes quiet and Bonhof to long range shooting, then we would have the measure of them. But, as it turned out, they had not come to play, merely to spoil and defend.

We kept plodding away at them but never cracked them open. It went into extra time and then came the dreaded penalties. They seemed happy enough to get to this stage and obviously fancied their chances. Kempes missed their first and we were on a high. Seconds later Liam missed his and we were back to apprehension. The next four penalties were scored by each side. Then it came to sudden death, all the effort of the past season riding on one kick. The Valencia player converted his kick and then it was Graham Rix's turn. The keeper guessed right and that was it. It all seemed so unbelievable – I really did feel for him and we all shared his disappointment. The 'highs' of beating Liverpool and Juventus were in sharp contrast to the 'lows' after West Ham and Valencia. After all we had gone through, it did not seem possible that we had won nothing. Things were really muted back at the hotel and nobody stayed around very long after the meal. What was even more incredible was that we still had two League games to play and needed to win both to qualify for Europe. We went to Wolves two days later and won 2-1. It was a credit to the players that we could keep going after the huge disappointments of the previous weeks. Our final game was at Middlesbrough three days later. We were trounced 5-0, and lucky to get away with that. The way everything had gone, it just had to happen like that, and the lads were well and truly ready for a holiday.

– 7 –

Arsenal 1980/81

The negotiations between Arsenal and Liam Brady had gone on a long time and seemed to be getting nowhere. Arsenal claimed that they were willing to make Liam the best paid player in England. I don't think the problem was down to Terry, he was desperate to keep Liam, but I felt his hands were tied by the directors. Liam, in the meantime, even spoke to Manchester United to try and secure the best deal for himself which was his right under freedom of contract. Eventually, Liam moved to Italy, but what I could not understand was that Terry Neill, not long after Liam had joined Juventus, signed Clive Allen for £1,000,000 and said if the club had not used the money they would have had to pay £400,000 in corporation tax. If they were really worried about paying the tax why not pay it to Liam, the best player in the country? I think it came down to Liam being at the club a long time and the directors believed that a young man should not be earning such large amounts of money particularly one that was working for them.

When Clive Allen signed for Arsenal, I wondered where he was going to play. The previous season Alan Sunderland and myself had scored fifty-one goals between us in all competitions. While it was always a priority to bring in another striker, I did not think that a one million pound player was going to be happy playing in the reserves. We played a friendly game against Luton at our training ground and all three of us were included in the team. I asked Terry what position each of us was playing and he replied, "The three of you just move about up front". We won the game 5-0 but it was obvious that playing three central strikers was not going to work. All sorts of combinations were tried in pre-season games. Clive was an out and out goal scorer whereas Alan and myself tended to share the workload and make runs all over the park. That's what was expected of Clive and it just was not in his make up. I don't blame Clive Allen one little bit as he was totally unsuited to the Arsenal style at that time. Clive never got to play a league game because he was transferred to Crystal Palace in exchange for Kenny Samson. It came as a shock to everyone inside and outside the club. To pay £1 million for a full back seemed a bit extravagant considering that usually all the million pound players were either a midfield or forward player. A defender is not going to win a game for you but Terry and Don saw it as a good signing which would improve the team, but there was no defender worth a million pounds in 1980.

When the season got under way, the starting line-up was different to that of the season before. We had two new full backs in Samson and Devine, Paul Vaessen was up front with me and John Hollins in midfield. Graham Rix now had the role of playmaker on the left side of midfield and a lot was expected of him.

It seemed strange for Liam Brady not to be there because he had been in the team all the time that I had played at Arsenal, but as Don had said on numerous occasions when the subject of Liam had arisen, Arsenal are bigger than any one player and it will survive the loss of Brady. People were again looking at us to do something after the near misses of last season but with three experienced players out of the team it was going to be a long hard season.

We won our first game away at West Brom and followed up with another win against Southampton at home. We had been well drilled in pre-season and we were very difficult to beat. We were always well organised and this was helping to alleviate the loss of Liam. This season the top two teams were Aston Villa and Ipswich and it seemed like a good opportunity to capitalise on Liverpool's inconsistency in the league. Again, we were always in the top six in the league and we were showing more consistency in our results but our performances were not as convincing as the previous season's. We were beaten by Tottenham in the fourth round of the League Cup, our first defeat in a local derby since I had made my debut in the first team, so it was a little unusual for our supporters to be out of a Cup so early. We still had a great team and the young players were getting better all the time, but crowds get impatient very quickly and can put the manager and the team under a lot of pressure.

There had been a lot of speculation in the papers that I would be going abroad at the end of the season when my contract was up. The stories were totally without foundation but still some of the stories obviously stayed in the supporter's minds as supporters would ask me what was happening and if I was leaving, as they had read so in the papers. My reply was always the same, I had no inclination to leave Arsenal and that I would talk to the club at the end of the season. Nevertheless there were times when I didn't play too well and certain sections of the crowd got on my back. This had never happened before and it was obvious that some were believing what they were reading.

In the twenty-five league games up to Christmas we had only lost five and had drawn ten, but it really wasn't good enough to win the Championship. Our problem was that we could beat the top sides but struggled against the lower teams like Birmingham and Sunderland, both of whom beat us at their grounds. We needed another creative midfield player to compliment Graham Rix. When Graham had played beside Liam they had played well together, changing positions regularly throughout games to lose markers and create chances, but it was all on the shoulders of Graham now and this was unfair. We were drawn away to Everton in the F.A. Cup and our dream of a fourth Cup final in a row, was gone when they beat us 2-0. It was now down to the league and to try and make an impact on the leaders.

But we lacked consistency again and after we lost 1-0 at Leicester, Terry bought Peter Nicholas from Crystal Palace with just nine games to go. He gave us a bit more bite and variety in midfield. In his first home game we beat Liverpool 1-0 and Peter Nicholas had made his mark after a late tackle on one of their players. It was only his second game but there was a transformation of the team and we went to the end of the season without a defeat. It was a pity, but there weren't enough games for us to catch the leader Aston Villa whom we had beaten in that run. What we really missed was Europe and the buzz it gave players and supporters. We had come third in the league and lost the same amount of games as the champions Aston Villa. It was the drawn games, fifteen in all, that had stopped us from winning the Championship. Qualification for Europe was assured, but first I had the problem of agreeing a new contract with the club.

My solicitor, Michael Kennedy had talks before the end of the season with the club, and negotiations were continuing slowly. I went away with the team to Hong Kong to play one match, and when I returned Don had a quiet word with me. I was a bit surprised because Don never got involved with players' contractual situations. He said he hoped I would stay and if there was a problem he would have a word on my behalf. I thought it was a really nice gesture and thanked him for it. I suppose he wanted to work with the best players available because it made his job easier. The ironic thing was that he said that his contract was up as well and if they could not come to an agreement he would be leaving!

The club made an offer which was not acceptable and it was just left like that until we returned for pre-season training. Whilst I was having a break in Ireland, I got a phone call to say that Liverpool wanted to speak to me, permission had been given by Arsenal so we arranged to meet in the Burlington Hotel, Dublin. Those present were John Smith the Chairman, Bob Paisley and Peter Robinson the Secretary. They outlined what they were looking for and said that the manager wanted me and he had the full backing of the board. I was very flattered and when we discussed terms they said there would not be any problem. I was impressed with the way they dealt with everything, they did not beat about the bush and if they were unable to do something they said so immediately. There was only one problem on their side and that was the transfer fee. They were going to try and part-exchange David Johnson and hoped Arsenal would be interested. It was all left at that and it was now up to the clubs to reach an agreement.

In action at Old Trafford against Wolverhampton Wanderers

– 8 –

From Arsenal To Manchester United
Pre-season 1981/82

I was at home in my parents' house in Ireland when the phone rang – it was a journalist from the *Daily Mirror*, Harry Miller. I thought that he was going to ask me about the transfer speculation at the time, but instead he said that the manager of Manchester United, Ron Atkinson wanted to speak to me and asked if I would go and speak to him in London that evening. I explained that I was getting married two days later and was busy making the arrangements for the ceremony. I asked him to phone back while I discussed it with Chris, my wife to be, to see what she thought of the situation. It was agreed that I would travel to London Airport and try to return on the last flight.

It was the first time I had met Ron Atkinson and my initial impression of him was that he was flash and full of himself. As time wore on I noticed that he appeared very insecure and unsure of himself in certain situations, and used mannerisms to try and hide these weaknesses. One thing he was sure of was that he was going to make Manchester United a team that played exciting football and get them back amongst the elite again. There was nothing finally agreed but it was now up to the club to take it further and contact Arsenal about a transfer fee, though there was no other representative of

Manchester United there that night. It was Ron Atkinson's responsibility to sell it to the Manchester United board.

As usually happens in these situations you don't hear anything for weeks and you begin to believe that nothing is going to happen. I had returned to London and began pre-season training as usual with Arsenal. Then out of the blue, Manchester United asked me to come up to Old Trafford to meet with the Chairman and other club representatives to discuss the details of the contract further and to bring my solicitor with me. The beginning of the season was getting closer and I was getting no match practice. After our discussions there was still no agreement and I returned to continue training at Arsenal. Arsenal had said all along that the contract they had offered me was the best in the club. I felt that they really believed that I would not leave, and the fact that I had grown up at the club would make me opt for them in the end.

David O' Leary was in exactly the same position as me and when the first team went to Sweden to play in a friendly match, we stayed behind to train with the reserves. It was a situation which had occurred twelve months earlier when Liam Brady had decided to leave. I don't think they realised how good he was for the team until after he had left.

There seemed to be a disagreement between the Club Secretary Ken Friar and Terry Neill about the terms that the club were offering, and Terry went directly to the Chairman to get permission to make a new offer. After waiting at Mr Friar's house, Terry turned up an hour and a half late with new terms which Ken Friar knew nothing about. As it turned out the terms came nowhere near Manchester United's and we were still back where we started. I never really wanted to leave Arsenal and had enjoyed my time there. It was the only club that I had known but I felt they were trying to take advantage of that loyalty and also of the fact that I had come through the club's system.

On the 14th August 1981 I signed for Manchester United but the clubs had failed to agree on the transfer fee. Arsenal wanted £2 million and United offered £700,000, so it went to a tribunal. Arsenal had felt aggrieved as they felt Manchester United should have approached them for permission to speak to me first. Under the freedom of contract rules they did not need to, but Arsenal felt it would have been a courtesy. The tribunal set the fee at £900,000, a record, and Arsenal insisted on the money being paid up front. I was glad to see the end of the whole affair so I could concentrate on what I was paid to do – play football.

What a relief! My first goal for Manchester United against Ipswich town
(Goalkeeper Paul Cooper)

— 9 —

Manchester United 1981/82

It was a relief to get our league campaign going after all the hulla-balloo that had gone on before. Nothing really matters unless the business is done on the pitch, and that is what the club had paid the record transfer fee for. Our first game was away at Coventry City and I found it difficult to adjust to the style of the team, partly because I had not played too many games in pre-season and felt that I lacked the sharpness that only games can give you. We ended up losing 2-1 but due to all the changes that occurred within the club, it was felt that it would take time for everything to blend. It had been a let down for the fantastic travelling support but the season was only just underway and we had two home matches in a row to come.

The game against Notts Forest was played on the Monday afternoon as it was a bank holiday, and over 51,000 people turned up with great expectations for the new United. But, they were let down, Forest had come to defend and catch us on the break and the game ended up scoreless. Most of the talk after the game was about Ron Atkinson wanting to sign Bryan Robson from his old club West Brom, but it was neither confirmed nor denied.

After our disappointing first two games, 45,655 people still turned up to see us play Ipswich the following Saturday. They were one of the top teams in the country at the time, with players like Butcher and Osman at the back, Muhrein and Thompson in midfield, and Mariner and Brazil up front. We went a goal down early in the game when Brazil got through and slipped the ball past Gary Bailey, but the crowd did not get on our backs, we were still trying to play football in the old United tradition. In the second half, I got my first goal for the club when I chased a long ball from Martin Buchan and lobbed it over their keeper for the equaliser. Just before the end, John Wark got their winner after a near post corner had been flicked on. So, after three games we had one point, and from the outside things looked gloomy, but as we had so many quality players at the club, Wilkins, McIlroy, Coppell, it was not a true reflection of how the team was playing. Manchester United is such a big club that success is taken for granted. The club has a reputation for attacking football and this must go hand in hand with winning trophies. I felt the manager was getting a little bit jittery after this latest set-back as it was a pressure situation he had never faced at his previous club West Brom. He threatened to make changes if we did not start getting results.

The main difference I found between Arsenal and Manchester United was the amount of press people about the club. At Arsenal you very rarely saw the press at either the ground or training ground. If, for instance, a reporter wanted to do a feature on any player he would usually go through the manager first, whereas at Manchester United the press were openly encouraged to write about the club or the players on a daily basis. On numerous occasions reporters would just turn up at a minutes notice and expect you to be available for an interview. This is all very fine when they are writing nice things about you or the club but you have no control if they want to write the opposite. Apparently, when Dave Sexton was manager, there were no press conferences held and they had to wait at the door of the training ground for the squad to be announced. Under Ron Atkinson the press were invited inside and treated to tea and biscuits. I think this was a sign of the insecurity which was evident when I first met Ron in London before I signed.

In our fourth league game at Aston Villa I scored again but we drew and had the honorous distinction of being bottom of the League. After that we played twelve league games without defeat and went to the top of the league. In the middle of that run we signed Bryan Robson and Remi Moses from West Brom, for two million pounds and the manager felt that he now had a squad that would take the title. In our seventh League game I went back to Highbury to play against my former club Arsenal. I got a very hot reception and was called a traitor and a money-grabber. I suppose in one way it was a compliment because supporters don't give you stick if they don't rate you. However, I was a little bit hurt because I had spent nine great years at the club and felt that I had been a little exploited as a youngster in the first team. I felt stronger- minded and more experienced to cope with the situation when the offer came from United.

This was in complete contrast to Liam Brady who had left to play abroad and was always accepted back with open arms whenever he came back to play in testimonials or friendly games at Highbury. In the supporters' eyes the worst transgression was not leaving the club but joining another "English" team.

When the Christmas period of games came around we were second in the League and seemed to have a more settled side, all the players adjusting to each other and blending into the pattern that was set. Garry Birtles was scoring freely and playing like he used to at Nottingham Forest. When I started playing with Garry I thought he was a very good player and I could not understand why he had not got the goals to complement the rest of his play. After a while I realised that he was getting too involved with the buildup and never found himself with too many scoring opportunities. I mentioned this to him a few times and once he got off the mark he was scoring regularly but also getting in the position to miss them.

In January we had a fairly average month losing in the third round of the F.A. Cup at Watford and losing to Swansea City at the Vetch Field in a match we had the chances to win. I knew that it was games like these which would count at the end of the season. Two wins at the beginning of February against Aston Villa 4-1 at home, and Wolves 1-0 away, kept us in the top three and as long as we did not drop silly points we were still on course. However, Liverpool were still just behind the leading pack and threatening to put a run of results together. Sammy McIlroy and Jimmy Nicholl both left the club to join Stoke City and Sunderland respectively. I think Ron Atkinson had made his mind up that these two players were not to be part of his plans. Sammy, I felt was unlucky because he had played well all season but the manager had to find places for Bryan Robson and Remi Moses and Sammy was the one to make the way. He was the last of Busby Babes at the club.

Our home form started to let us down – we drew with both Arsenal and Manchester City. Maybe it was the pressure of playing at Old Trafford but we seemed inhibited as a team and were playing better football away from home. We beat Birmingham City away 1-0 with a goal from Garry Birtle, but the flowing football that we had shown earlier in the season was not coming through. But if the team is not playing well and getting results, there is still a chance of winning something once you get through the bad patch.

Our next home match brought the low point of the season. We were playing Coventry City and could not put any consistency into our passing and then the inevitable happened. Terry Gibson scored the only goal of the match for Coventry City . At the end we were booed off and I suppose the only good thing that you could say was that it was from the lowest crowd of the season. We had really blown our chance of winning the championship and teams who were struggling were giving us the hardest games. We knew that any team that played against Manchester United always lifted their game but that's what makes anyone who plays for United and can cope, a special player. We bounced back with a 3-1 win at Notts County but let ourselves down again with a 0-0 draw at home to Sunderland.

Our next home game was the biggest in the supporters' eyes. It was against Liverpool and there was over 48,000 people there, to hopefully record the double for the season. After five minutes we got a penalty and at that time I was taking them. I put the ball to Grobblear's left but he guessed the right way and knocked it round the post. We ended up losing 1-0 and I felt like my whole world was crumbling. If it had gone in I think we would have gone on to win quite comfortably. I could not help noticing afterwards in the match programme, a picture of me taking a penalty the week before in a friendly match, and putting it to the same side. I learnt afterwards that he had seen the picture and decided to go the same way – talk about inside information! In our last five home matches we had lost two and drawn three – definitely not championship material.

What was galling, from the players point of view, was that there was no lack of effort. We had international players on the team but the manager did not seem to be able to give us that little something that would get us out of the rut, he seemed to think that because we had so much experience it would just happen, though I think every player needs help at some time during their career. There was also criticism of the players by the manager in the press and this definitely did not help the situation. As I said before, I think the right place for criticism is in the dressing room and that is where it should stay, but to openly criticise the players in the press showed a lack of respect for us as people and professionals.

At this time, Liverpool had surged to the top of the table and were in the middle of an unbeaten run. There were ten games left and we really had to pull out all the stops to catch them. In those ten games we won seven, drew two and lost one, but it still was not good enough. It was still a fairly successful season even though we did not win a trophy. I played in forty-one league games and only missed the last one because of injury, making way for a young lad called Norman Whiteside who was to make even bigger headlines a month later by being the youngest player ever to appear in the World Cup finals. The manger looked set to bring in more new players for the new season and if that was so, it would make our squad as competitive as any in the country. We had qualified for Europe, which was important to the club because of the prestige and to the players as they had to pit their wits and skills against top continental opposition. Not winning the league had been a disappointment to everyone at the club. It was felt that the team still had to develop fully but it was the manner in which the team had played – attacking and minding, which was the philosophy of the manager. Everyone was looking forward to the new season with expectations higher than they were a year previously.

But it wasn't all gloom, there was one funny story which I remembered from the season and it was aimed at the manager by Martin Buchan, whose wit can be very cruel if you to take it seriously. The team were in Spain for a pre-season tournament when the players went outside to have a look at the pitch. We were in the centre circle when Ron Atkinson came along and said to Martin, "Have you ever played here before?" Martin replied, "Yes, when you were starring in the 3rd division with Oxford." Needless to say Martin did not play in the tournament!

– 10 –

Wembley Glory Again 1982/83

As with every pre-season at Manchester United there was a lot of speculation in the press that we would be signing new players – every day there was a new name. One player the manager definitely did sign was Arnold Muhren from Ipswich and Holland (it was said that his left foot could open a can of peas!). As most players will agree the pre-season is the most important part of the season as it gives you the power and stamina to keep going through a long hard season. After the first week's training and one friendly match against Aldershot, we flew out to Iceland to play some games. I ended up injuring my ankle in the first game and spent the next two weeks trying to get the swelling down. More importantly, I was missing valuable pre-season training and games which help you get that vital match fitness for the start of the season.

While I was out of the team they had won a pre-season tournament in Saragosa, Spain and had scored eight goals in two games. Most notable of the scorers was Garry Birtles who scored three of the goals. All the talk through pre-season had been about Garry going back to Notts Forest but if he kept this up, the manager would have to think again. The emergence of Norman Whiteside during the World Cup had prompted these rumours and with Norman also playing well it was going to be interesting. A week before the season Remi Moses, Steve Coppell and myself all played against Arsenal reserves at the Cliff to test out our injuries and with one more game before the season started it was going to be close.

We started off the season on a high note beating Birmingham City 3-0, both Steve Coppell and myself getting on the score sheet. There was a feeling of optimism in the club and also, in the team, that we were going to win something. The team was full of international players and if we could keep everyone fit we had a real chance of winning the league title. Our second game ended with the same scoreline at Notts Forest with all our ability coming through, playing delightful attacking football. Garry Birtles signed for Forest after the game for £250,000 – £1 million less than was paid for him. All the players were sad to see Garry go because he was popular in the dressing room. He used to wear outrageous clothes and Ray Wilkins nicknamed him 'Baggy Jagger' but I think Garry was happy that he was back in his native Nottingham again.

Our early season form was very good, losing one game out of six. Norman Whiteside was a revelation, he was scoring freely, whilst I was struggling to find my form. He was carrying me in those early games and I put it down to missing those two important weeks in pre-season. Our form had pushed us to top of the league but we were only one point ahead of Liverpool who also had a good start. In the European Cup we drew Valencia and the first leg was at home. The Spaniards came for a draw, and kicked their way to it, but had four players booked en route. They got the draw they came for and went home happy but we felt we were a better footballing side and could win over there. On the second leg we went one up but conceded two goals late in the game to send us out. In the League Cup we went through 4-2 on aggregate against Bournemouth but there was bad news – Ray Wilkins was taken to hospital with a stress fracture of the cheekbone and would be out for three months. It was a real setback for us because Ray was the one who made us play and enabled Bryan Robson to get forward into the box. I had been going through a goal-scoring famine but I didn't feel that I was playing badly. The manager had been critical in the newspapers and I felt it was unfair. If the manager had called me into his office and criticised me, then I would have accepted it as long as it was kept within the confines of his office. The one thing one never saw at Liverpool was the manager publicly criticising his players – if it was good enough for them it was good enough for us. Being manager at Manchester United meant that there had to be something about the club everyday in the paper. I think Big Ron got a little carried away with what they were saying and started to believe things attributed to him in the papers.

Over the next two months we had been very inconsistent losing away games to teams in the bottom half of the table like West Ham and Brighton, but our home form was good in contrast to the previous season and we were battling more for results this season than we were last. Our biggest problem had been scoring, not just the strikers but the whole team. Maybe it was the fact that we had not played with a natural wide man since Steve Coppell had been injured but Norman and myself were big front players and therefore relied on good service from the wings. When the Christmas period of games came, we did not score in four of the five games and the critics were once again critical of the forwards. To be fair to the manager he said the responsibility was on the team's shoulders.

When the F.A. Cup came round we were playing West Ham at home. Steve Coppell had worked hard to get himself back to the fitness level that he had shown before his knee operation. It had been a stop-start season for him and now he felt he was right on song again. There was a great atmosphere for the Cup tie – a real air of expectancy because the club had a great tradition in the F.A. Cup. We won a great game 2-0 with Steve and myself getting the goals, but, more importantly, we had won with a good performance from the team. Things were starting to boil up nicely for the season – quarter-final of the League Cup, fourth round of the F.A. Cup and still in a good position in the League with nineteen Championship games to go.

In the next two months we played as many Cup ties as league games. In the League Cup we beat Notts. Forest 4-0 and then met Arsenal in a two-legged semi-final. It was a big game for me in every way, I had left Arsenal to win trophies elsewhere and after this tie was over it would go some way to proving my point. Everyone believed that we would go there for a draw but we played the best football since I had joined the club. The Gunners did not know what had hit them, the manager had told us not to sit back but to take the game to them. We were 4-0 up midway through the second half, but they pulled two goals back in the last fifteen minutes to give some respectability to the score line. Our football had been unbelievable and they just couldn't cope with us on the night. It was a great reward for our travelling support who had been frustrated on so many occasions that season. Personally, I was very happy having shoved the stick I had got all night from the terraces back down their throats. We were now on the verge of Wembley, we shouldn't lose with a two goal lead and home advantage. In the second match they gave us some early scares but we came through 2-1 in the end and booked our place at Wembley. The crowd on the night was over 56,000 which meant nearly 100,000 people had watched the two games. This was one of the big highlights of playing for a big club like United, there were always big crowds home and away and the atmosphere was great.

In the F.A. Cup we had beaten Luton and Derby away to earn a home quarter-final tie against Everton. Our unbeaten run in the League had come to a halt at Stoke and we had fallen a long way behind Liverpool who had been beaten in the F.A. Cup by Brighton and were on an unbeaten run in the league. By this time our concentration was definitely in the Cup competitions with the possibility of two Wembley appearances.

We met Liverpool in the League Cup final in what was always going to be a hard match. We were without Bryan Robson who had been out for a while and was just not ready on the day. Nevertheless with a midfield of Moses, Wilkins and Muhren we had enough ability to cause Liverpool more than a few problems. After twelve minutes Norman scored a fabulous goal, turning Alan Hansen, and shooting with his right foot into the corner. It stayed like that until half-time but nothing could have prepared us for what was to happen in the second half.

Kevin Moran had to go off with an ankle injury and six minutes later, Liverpool were level, with Alan Kennedy scoring from twenty-five yards. Gordon McQueen then picked up an injury and moved up front, I took his position at the back but people were going down with all sorts of injuries as the game neared the end of ninety minutes. The game went into extra time with our back four of Macari, Stapleton, Duxbury and Albiston but we kept battling on with ten men. We were frustrating Liverpool, but it was only going to be a matter of time before something happened. I went to close down Ronnie Whelan about twenty-five yards out and he tried to pass the ball through my legs. I blocked it but it ran straight back to him and he curled an unstoppable shot into the top corner past Gary Bailey. That was the lowest point of the season for me after putting so much into the match, and the fact that injuries had robbed us of victory didn't help.

In the dressing room, all heads were down. It was pointed out that we still had a chance of coming back in a month's time but the obstacle of Arsenal had to be overcome (again). On the way home there was a great resolve to get back to Wembley but to be winners this time. Two weeks before, we had beaten Everton 1-0 in the last minute. They had missed two great chances to put the game beyond our reach, when, with a minute to go Ron Atkinson threw on Lou Macari for Mike Duxbury. With the very last attack of the match Ray Wilkins sent a long ball to Macari who headed it down to me and I volleyed it into the far corner. The noise that erupted at that moment was the loudest I have ever heard, it was the most important goal I had scored for Manchester United to date. They kicked-off but the game was over – we were in the semi-final of the F.A. Cup.

Once again, our League form dipped and we were falling further behind Liverpool but our best performances were kept for the Cup ties. The semi-final had everything you could ask for with both teams desperate to get to the final. Arsenal scored first through Tony Woodcock and held the lead up to half-time. The team showed great resilience and character as Bryan Robson equalised for us. Then it looked as if fate was going to take over again when Kevin Moran went off with a cut head. This time we made sure that fate played no part with a fantastic volley by Norman Whiteside which gave their goalkeeper George Wood no chance. The supporters had lifted the players when we needed it most and we went on to to reach Wembley again.

In the dressing room Kevin had once again had his head stitched and was in the bath when some of the lads decided to throw the coach, Mick Brown, in. Unfortunately, he landed on Kevin and opened up his stitches, so he had to go and have them redone.

We had eight League games left and no chance of winning the Championship but we still had to play well to maintain our form for the final. The results were not consistent – in our last game at Notts County we were 2-1 in front with ten minutes to go and they ended up winning 3-2. Because of that defeat we missed runners-up spot and the manager was not happy at all.

The buildup to the Cup final was all about the television and press constantly being around doing interviews. The manager was in his element – whenever a television camera appeared he was there, but the players tried to have a normal routine and carried on regardless. A lot of what goes on is just hype but the Final is such a media attraction throughout the world, some things are contrived to fill up their newstime. It is still a great feeling being involved but the most important thing is the match which of course has to be won. A team's form in the league is no real indicator because it is a one-off situation and anything can happen on the day.

On the day of the final it was raining and had been constantly doing so for nearly twenty-four hours. The pitch was soggy, but the weather did not dampen the enthusiasm of the supporters who looked really colourful. We seemed to have 70 per cent of the support except for the end where the tunnel is. The team was as expected, with just one change, Alan Davies who was in for only his fourth senior appearance in place of Steve Coppell.

The game started and we were hardly in our stride when Gordon Smith gave Brighton the lead after fourteen minutes. We were looking sluggish, particularly at the back, and were not as tight on their forwards as we should have been. We didn't get an equaliser before half-time and Brighton went in with their tails up. The manager impressed on us what we had done to get here and if we didn't improve the game would pass us by and we would lose it.

After the break, our play did improve and after a Mick Duxbury centre was flicked on by Norman Whiteside I got to the ball off the far post to ram it into the net. It was the second time I had scored in a Wembley Cup final and it put the record straight as far as United were concerned. Immediately, we started to play like our old selves.

Eighteen minutes from the end, Ray Wilkins scored a brilliant goal to give us the lead and we looked to have won the game. But the F.A. Cup is full of fairy tales and ten minutes from time Brighton scored the equaliser. The match then went into extra time. With seconds to go in extra time Brighton broke away and Gordon Smith had the chance to win the Cup, but Gerry Bailey stopped the ball with his legs. We were still in with a chance. At that moment, I thought that that was the end for us and I was close to feeling how United felt four years previously against Arsenal.

When we stepped out the following Thursday for the replay, every player knew that we had got away with a draw, and we were going to make sure there was no mistake this time. It was a different game this time – we were 3-0 up at half-time with goals from Bryan Robson (2) and Norman Whiteside. Arnold Muhren scored a penalty in the second half to give us the biggest winning margin in a Wembley Final.

The journey home was something very special. The club had hired a train to take us back to Manchester. On the train were directors, family, friends and all the staff at Old Trafford. It was only right that they should share in the glory of winning because they had all played their part throughout the season. It was also nice that we won the Cup on Sir Matt Busby's birthday. After all the ups and downs of the season it was a great ending and one I will never forget.

Celebrating my goal against Everton (L. to R. Gordon McQueen, myself, Arnold Muhren and Lou McCarry)

– 11 –

Manchester United 1983/84

After the euphoria of winning the Cup, a lot of people felt this could be our year to land the big prize, the League Championship, but we had been tipped every year and the winning had to be done on the pitch. The competition for places in the team was fiercer than ever, from the back to the front, yet only one player had been bought, Arthur Graham from Leeds United for £45,000. In midfield there was real competition with Bryan Robson, Remi Moses, Ray Wilkins and Arnold Muhren vying for three positions but a nice problem for the manager. There was cover in almost every position but the manager was still on the lookout for new players. According to the papers Manchester United were interested in every player that became available though I thought he would have to be exceptional because of the calibre of players at the club.

Being the Cup winners we were involved in the Charity Shield against Liverpool at Wembley. It was our fourth visit in six months and it was an indicator of how we would play after last season. We had no injury problems this time and deservedly ran out 2-0 with goals by Bryan Robson. Beating Liverpool had always been normal for Manchester United but it was in the league when we were against bread and butter opposition that we always seemed to fall down. I think this was a combination of two things: firstly, that the opposition always raised their game and secondly, that Manchester United were always expected to attack, home or away, and very rarely, in my time there did we shut up shop and kill the game off, something which Liverpool were masters at.

Victorious in the Charity Shield.
L. to R. Watkins, Duxbury, Robson, Bailey, Moses, Graham, Wheelan, Whiteside, McCarry.
Front Row: myself, F.S. Gidmen, McQueen, Albiston, Muhren, Moran.

We started off our League campaign at home with a 3-1 win over QPR. Two days later, again at home to Notts Forest, we were coasting 1-0 up and playing delightful football but we let them in for two goals in the last ten minutes to lose a game we had totally dominated. This was the sort of thing that had stopped us in the previous season. We quickly made up for it with two away victories at Stoke and Arsenal, the latter with me scoring in front of the North Bank who had been giving me stick from the first whistle and it made the victory even sweeter. We then beat Luton 2-0 at home and we were well placed in the league after five matches.

We had drawn Dukla Prague in the Cup Winners Cup with the first leg at home. Manchester United had never lost a European match at home but we looked like losing it when the Czech's scored a breakaway goal and we never looked like pulling it back. There was a minute to go when I chased a long ball from Arthur Albiston, there was no real danger but the goalkeeper came rushing out and took my feet as I went past him and gave us a penalty. Ray Wilkins duly obliged to the relief of everyone in the stadium. Things did not look bright for us with an away goal conceded and a tough game in Prague in a fortnight.

I felt that the manager, Ron Atkinson had been very cocky since we had won the Cup. He had been a real "Jack the lad", coming out with sarcastic remarks to players when they had an off day. He was also creating an image for himself with television, commentating on live matches. We would not see him for most of the week but if the cameras were there he would turn up and have his hair groomed so that he looked his best. There was no doubt he had a big ego, but he also had a good relationship with the press who liked to deal with him because he would give them lots of quotes and stories. He called me in once and asked me if I knew Eamonn Dunphy, I said I did, but did not like the guy. Seemingly he had done an article on Ron criticising him and a lot of what was in the article had obviously come from within the club and he had thought that I had supplied the information. He had no foundation for accusing me, but he knew that I would not take any such accusation.

We were doing well in the League and our form was good with Arthur Graham – a revelation. Both Norman Whiteside and myself had benefited immensely from his supply of crosses and the style of play of the team had helped him also. I had scored the winner against Liverpool, but Arthur Graham had created it by getting to the by-line and whipping over a great cross. We then went to Prague and it turned out to be a great open game, we got a 2-2 draw which put us through to the next round on away goals. A funny incident occurred with five minutes to go. Arthur Graham picked the ball up in his own half, proceeded to beat players and was showing great urgency. We were screaming at him to try and get the ball back to Gary Bailey but Arthur thought we had to score another goal to win the game! In the next round we played Spartak Varna who were beaten in both legs and we were through to the quarter-finals which were to be played in March.

Going into the New Year we were three points behind Liverpool with the game at Anfield, our first of the New Year to come. We came away with a 1-1 draw, so everything stayed the same. Our defence of the F.A. Cup began at Bournemouth and that is where it ended. It was a disaster for us, and each one of us was a disgrace. We were beaten by a very ordinary team who wanted to win more than us and we were slaughtered by the press but had no comeback. There was an air of depression at the club all the week as it had been the second time this season we had lost to a lower division team – Oxford having knocked us out of the League Cup. The next game was going to be a real test of character, but we managed to get a draw at QPR and keep our momentum going in the league. We got the Cup result out of our systems and began to play again with confidence. We played eleven games without losing, culminating in a 4-0 defeat of Arsenal at

Old Trafford to put us two points ahead in the league, with ten games to go. Our next game at Notts Forest was postponed so we had a free week. The manager wanted to take a trip to Spain but the players said they would prefer to stay at home and keep the momentum going, but the manager went ahead regardless and the players were made to go on a trip they did not want.

We duly lost our next game to West Brom, the sequence was broken and we never did reach the peak we had in the Arsenal game. It was a shame because at the time the players believed they could win every match that was left.

In Europe we drew Barcelona who had Maradonna and Schuster on their side. Away we had played well and lost to an O.G. and a screaming shot in the last minute. It was a daunting task to pull two goals back, but we knew Old Trafford would be full and the crowd would make it as uncomfortable as possible for the Spaniards. The atmosphere was fantastic as 58,500 people came to see if we could turn the tie our way. When Bryan Robson pulled two goals back in the first half the place just erupted – it was the best atmosphere I have ever experienced at Old Trafford. In the second half we were pressing and pressing for the winner and when Norman Whiteside headed on Arnold Muhren's cross down, I volleyed what turned out to be the winning goal. The noise was deafening, the results against Bournemouth and Oxford a blur, and everybody was dancing and cheering. Graham Hogg who was only in his first season in the first team marked Maradona completely out of the game. It was a night to remember at Old Trafford.

In the semi-final we drew Juventas but bad luck hit us again when our midfield of Robson, Wilkins and Muhren were all ruled out of the first match. With our engine room out we could only manage a 1-1 draw at home but performed well under the circumstances. They had the away goal but I hoped that history was going to repeat itself from four years earlier when the result was the same after the first leg.

The second leg was electric, there were firecrackers and smoke flares everywhere and the stadium was full. It was the situation most players dream of playing in and it was going to be a big test. The Italians were more adventurous, mainly due to the fact that they had Michel Platini and Boniek on their team. Platini was dictating the play and we couldn't get near him on the night. They went ahead through Boniek in the first half but Norman Whiteside equalised in the second half and it looked like going to extra time. A minute from the end a deflected shot fell to the feet of Paolo Rossi and we were out of the Cup.

We had five games to go in the league but our form was poor and we lost two and drew three. It had been our best chance of overcoming Liverpool but we had blown it in games where we had poor opposition. We had taken ten points out of the last thirty and ended up finishing in fourth place. It was a very disappointing season.

There was a close season tour arranged to Hong Kong and Australia but Ireland also had a trip to Japan.

I had a clause in my contract that stated that I would be released for all Ireland matches. The club were insisting that I go on the tour, yet were allowing the English internationals to come back straight after the first match in Hong Kong to play for England. I insisted that they agree to release me as it said in my contract. Big Ron was fuming because he was used to bullying people to get his own way but I stood firm and went to Japan with Ireland. Ray Wilkins was allowed to leave the club and join A.C. Milan. It was a great disappointment to me because Ray was a close friend and he had also been brilliant all season, but he was going from one great club to another. I thought that we should have been buying their players rather than the other way around.

– 12 –

Manchester United 1984/85

My situation with the club did not improve after I came back from the tour with Ireland injured. I had been feeling a strain on my thigh all through the tour so I decided to see the club doctor when I got back. He immediately sent me to see a specialist who said I would have to go into hospital for an exploratory operation on my knee to find out exactly what the problem was. He found a calcification of the thigh bone above my knee and it meant that I would not be able to train for three months.

In the meantime the club had invested in the transfer market, signing Gordon Strachan from Aberdeen, Jesper Olsen from Ajax and Alan Brazil from Tottenham. The signing of these players meant that the pattern of the team would change. There would be two wide players who could either link up with the front players or get to the byline to cross the ball. The signings had created a lot of excitement at Old Trafford – the fact that they were all attacking players was probably the reason. I was not allowed to start training until September, which meant that I would not be match fit until well into the season.

The team had started the season with four draws but it was the manner of the performances which was important, and the team soon picked up with good wins by five and three goals to show that there were plenty of goalscorers throughout the team. It meant that it was going to be difficult for me to get back in the team. Mark Hughes had forced his way into the team and he was keeping Norman Whiteside on the bench. I got my first chance when I came on as substitute against Everton but we lost 5-0 and it also reminded me of how much work I still had to do before I could regain the form that was going to keep me on the team. It was a frustrating time because I was watching the lads battling away in games and I wanted to be out there but I knew I had a long way to go. With Mark Hughes and Gordon Strachan scoring freely I was on and out of the team. I could not find any consistency and it was to be February before I got a chance to play against my old club. The manager called me in the day before the game and said that he was going to play me. I played my best game of the season. Norman Whiteside came on in a new midfield role which seemed to suit him perfectly. He ran the game when he came on and scored the winning goal. The manager had stumbled on something which was to make Norman a better player in a new position, which used his strength and aggression with his ability, for the teams greater benefit. It set us on a run of league games which saw us lose only three times until the end of the season but the F.A. Cup was also in our sights again.

In Europe we had reached the quarter-finals but not without some heart-stopping moments along the way.

Raba Gyor from Hungary were seen off quite comprehensively in the first round but P.S.V. Eindhoven proved a tougher nut to crack and were finally overcome with a penalty by Gordon Strachan in extra time. In the third round we drew Dundee United and handed them two goals in a match that we should have won 5-0 but it ended up 2-2. We went to Scotland to try to beat a team who had never been beaten at home in Europe. Again we came up trumps and won 3-2 to record an historic win. In the quarter-finals we again drew a Hungarian team, so it was going to be a matter of breaking them down and getting a good enough lead to take to the second leg. We had two goals disallowed on the night and only took a 1-0 lead to Hungary. They had not shown too much on the night, but in Europe that does not mean a thing and teams are totally transformed when they play at home. In the second leg, we arrived to play on a very windy night and the crowd was packed into a tiny little stadium. They did not shout too much at the start of the game, as we expected them to, putting us under a little pressure for the first twenty minutes. We were taking the game to them and finding more openings than in the first leg. Then disaster struck – they scored on a breakaway and the aggregate scores were level. From then on they were happy to get everyone back and kick the ball anywhere.

It was obvious that they were playing to get to penalties and after 120 minutes it came down to that. Both myself and Mark Hughes missed and they converted all but one of theirs. It was one of those occasions when you wished that the ground would open up and swallow you. The best team doesn't always win the penalty shoot out when all the effort of the previous rounds is decided on one kick.

Our next game after our European exit was at home to Aston Villa and we needed a win to stop our season from falling apart. It was a real test of character but we came through with flying colours winning 4-0, all the frustrations of the previous Wednesday being finally let out. It was a badly needed victory because we faced Liverpool at Anfield in our next game in front of the cameras. There was always great rivalry when the two clubs met, but more so because we were both still in with a chance of the League and the F.A. Cup. We came away with a 1-0 win and that gave us a psychological boost for the semi-final match in the Cup two weeks later. We were running into fine form just at the right time, though Everton had a strong lead in the League. The club was buzzing at this time, there were so many people around for autographs and watching training. It was all very enjoyable – and we were in with a chance of a trophy.

We had to play Liverpool at Goodison Park because they had been drawn out of the hat first. The atmosphere in the ground was fantastic and the football was just as good. We were playing our best football of the season and deservedly went ahead through a goal by

Mark Hughes. We were totally outplaying them and our supporters got right behind us. It seemed just a matter of time before we would add to our lead but Liverpool came out for the second half and equalised. I restored our lead not long afterwards and it looked like we were on our way to the final. There was about thirty seconds left when Dalgliesh crossed a hopeful ball. It seemed ages in the air but Gary Bailey had not come for it, Ian Rush headed the ball back and Paul Walsh ran it over the line. We had never appeared to be in danger, yet it was back to 2-2. We kicked off and the whistle blew for the end of the game. When we got in the dressing room, I had a blazing row with Gary Bailey. I said he should have come for the cross but he said it was too far out. The argument continued for ten minutes.

During all this time, the manager just stood there smiling. He was disappointed with the result but delighted with the performance. We were so wound up after the game that we just let everything out.

The replay was at Maine Road and we had majority support in the ground. Again there was a unique atmosphere but there was no guarantee that we could reproduce the form we had shown on the Saturday. On the night, after going a goal down we came back with goals from Bryan Robson and Mark Hughes to reach the final for the second time in three years. It was a great victory, although it could have been so different, because Liverpool rarely give you a second chance. Thankfully, it had all worked out in the end.

While our form in the league remained good, it was more obvious by the week of the final that Everton would win it because they had been the most consistent team all season and also their lead was unassailable. With the league championships under their belt we were the team who stood in their way for the coveted double, but it was our chance of winning a trophy and we were just as determined as they were.

The week of the Cup final was very subdued, mainly because of the horrendous fire at Bradford City's ground which had killed a number of people. It tended to bring home the fact that football, after all, was only a game, and on a list of things that are important in life, football is way down.

On the morning of the final both Kevin Moran and I woke up at seven o'clock which is unusual because we normally have to be roused from sleep on the morning of a game. We were both tense and both of us felt it was a good sign, rather than being too relaxed and not having the edge for the game. It was a hot day, as most F.A. Cup final days are, and energy had to be conserved. The game itself was a big disappointment. Both sides were pushing up to the half-way line and making it very difficult for fluent play, but there was so much at stake that neither team was willing to give an inch, which meant that both teams were cancelling each other out. The game was drifting towards extra time when the referee changed the whole course of the game. Peter Reid had intercepted a pass in midfield when Kevin Moran came across to tackle him but missed the ball and caught the player. It was a foul, but was just a mis-timed tackle as every player on the park agreed, but the referee took out the red card and sent Kevin off. It was the first time anyone had been sent off in an F.A. Cup final. The referee would not hear anything from the players and totally ignored all pleas from both sides. I think he made a big mistake, it was his last match and people would now remember him.

It was just the lift we needed as a team. I went back to play beside Paul McGrath and we all had to give that little bit extra to make up for the loss of a man. The game went into extra time and we were still holding our own when a long ball was played in. I fortunately headed it clear to Brian Robson who sprayed a ball out to Norman Whiteside on the right. As he made his way towards goal he feigned to play the ball and then curled a great shot past Southall into the corner of the net. It was a top quality goal and one to grace any final – but there was still time for them to equalise. The game seemed to go on for ever but it was the sweetest sound I had ever heard when the referee blew the final whistle. We had won against all the odds and maybe – no one will ever know – if Kevin Moran had not been sent off it might have gone to a replay and we might not have won at all!

Two weeks after the Cup final I was playing with Ireland in Dublin, when I got a phone call from an agent who said that he represented Bordeaux who played in the French first division. He said he would like to meet me, along with officials of the club, to discuss transferring me to them. I said that he should contact Manchester United as I was under contract. His reply was that a fee of £500,000 had been agreed between the clubs and they would come and meet me in Dublin. I was shocked and surprised but agreed to meet them when the game was over. They came over in their club jet and we sat down to try and work out a deal. The President was very dramatic, getting annoyed and agitated one minute and then calm and collected the next. It was all part of the way they negotiated and tried to put you under pressure. We could not agree on terms – it was a big decision to move to a foreign country and the terms they offered were not good enough to compensate for that, so we said our goodbyes and went our separate ways.

On the morning I got back to Manchester, the phone rang and it was the agent I had met. He wanted me to fly out to Bordeaux the next day and have a look around. I told him that I was going into hospital the next day to have my tonsils out and that it would be impossible for me to make the trip for at least a couple of weeks. I thought that was the end of that but the phone went a few minutes later and it was Ron Atkinson. He asked me what I was playing at, said that the terms offered were very good, and that I should go to Bordeaux as they requested. I said the terms were not good enough and that I was going to have my tonsils out the next day and that was that. He was not very happy and finished our conversation by slamming the phone down. He was desperate for me to go, but I was adamant, and stayed where I was. I felt sure it had a lot to do with what happened a year previously.

– 13 –
Manchester United 1985/86

Football was under the microscope after the terrible disaster at Bradford and the horrific events at Heysel Stadium in Brussels when thirty-nine Juventus fans were killed, after rival fans started fighting before the European Cup final. The game was at its lowest ebb for years; hooliganism had caused people to stay away from football and the game was fighting for its life. English football was seen to have the worst fans in the world and whenever there was trouble at matches the whole situation was blown out of proportion by the press. The season started off with added pressure on managers and players to produce more entertainment, and improved behaviour on the field.

We had been stuttering through our pre-season games and failing to find our real form. I felt we had reported back a little late for pre-season training and had not reached the right level of fitness by the time we played Everton in the Charity Shield at Wembley, a week before the season began. In that game they were yards faster than us and we were lucky to get away with a 2-0 defeat. In the following week the training was stepped up but no one could have foreseen the sort of start to the season we were going to have. Two new players were bought – John Sivbeck and Colin Gibson – to give the squad strength in depth. My relationship with the manager had not improved and I knew that I would have to play well to stay on the team because I was not his favourite person.

Our first game was at home to Aston Villa and for the first forty-five minutes we struggled to make any impact, and as we went in at half-time the crowd were getting restless. There had been a lot of tension in our game and the passes were going astray far too often. At the beginning of the second half we got the breakthrough and from there on, the football just flowed and we ran out winners, 4-0. This was to start us on an amazing run, winning ten straight games on the trot.

The funny thing about it was that there had been no tactical change resulting in this turnabout. The football we played in those matches was the best and most fluent of any team I had played in. The goals were coming from all departments of the team and the next game could not come quick enough. But the sign of any good manager or coach is the ability to get things back on the rails when they go wrong. Our run of games ended when we were beaten at Sheffield Wednesday.

We had come into the winter months and the pitches were getting heavier. It was making it more difficult to play the fluent football we had been playing earlier in the season. The manager did not know how to put it right. His way was to go out and buy somebody new in the hope that they would spark the team back into action. After we had lost a ten point lead there was all sorts of speculation in the papers about who was going to join us. In early January we travelled away to play at Oxford and it had been rumoured that Mark Hughes was going to leave to play for Barcelona. This had been strongly denied all week by the club but when we got up on Saturday morning it was all over the papers and was confirmed by the manager. The news overshadowed the match that day and even though Mark scored, it was going to be a heavy burden for him to carry for the rest of the season. A couple of weeks later Terry Gibson was bought from Coventry City. He had scored on a couple of visits to Old Trafford but I don't think that merited coming to play in a cauldron every other week. Terry was used to playing on a team that liked to play the ball over the top early and he was not going to get that sort of service with this team. Also, Peter Davenport was bought from Notts Forest. That meant things had got on top of Mark Hughes and he was struggling to keep his form, but the manager was not going to jeopardise a £2 million transfer by leaving him out. It was then that I realised that the money was more important than the championship.

Our form was poor but we had still got to the fifth round of the Cup at West Ham, where we had a 1-1 draw, to take them back to our place. The replay summed up our season – we lost 2-0 to a team who thought they had lost their chance by not winning the first game. The team was being changed every week in the hope that we could put a run of results together, but the secret of the run at the start of the season was that the team had been the same for the whole of the run. We had not scored nearly as many goals both as a team or individually and the confidence gained from those early games had evaporated. We were trailing the leaders, Liverpool and Everton, by a long way. The off the field goings on had not helped and we had not played as well as the previous season and the supporters saw it as another championship thrown away.

The manager was under pressure for his job but the Chairman had stood by him and had not gone with the media pressure but it had been the players as much as the manager who had brought this about. I felt my time at the club was coming to an end with so many new players, particularly forwards being signed up. I did not want to leave but I did not fancy playing reserve team football. I had been substituted six games on the trot, and the seventh game was a televised game against Sheffield Wednesday. The manager named the team but said he would name his substitute before the game. On the way home I was listening to the radio when the team was announced – I had been substituted with Terry Gibson. It was this sort of thing which was making the situation worse, telling the press but not bothering to tell the players involved.

We lost the game 2-0 at home and it was then that the manager decided to switch Mark Hughes to the left wing, but by then we were out of the title race. We went to Newcastle and won 4-2 and Mark Hughes scored two cracking goals but it was too little too late. I don't blame the player one little bit, I just think the team was sacrificed for the transfer money. What had started so well just ended with us getting into a modest fourth position, but it was not only what happened on the pitch that had made the season go like it had.

– 14 –
My United Farewell 1986/87

During the close season I had a long think about my position at the club and decided not to get involved in arguments with the manager but to buckle down and try and keep my place in the team by scoring and playing well. Things did not go well in the pre-season games, particularly when we went to Amsterdam for a tournament. We had played Dynamo Kiev on the Friday night and drew the game 1-1 but won the penalty shoot out. The next day we trained in the morning and were given the afternoon free to go around Amsterdam, but had to be back by six o'clock for dinner. Seven players didn't return until nine-thirty and they were all fined two weeks wages and did not play in the second game the next day against Ajax. Jasper Olsen had actually got into a fight with a taxi driver and ended up with a black eye. The manager decided to keep the story quiet and just get on with our preparation for the new season. Because the club is so big and has so many employees this news was bound to come out sooner or later. The pre-season was not too good but there was still a chance for things to pick up before the league programme started.

The first match of the season was away to Arsenal – always a difficult fixture. We lost it to a last minute goal and had played well on the day. The local reporter from the *Manchester Evening News*, David Meek, had reported about the incident in Amsterdam but just said that seven players had been fined and did not name them. Our next two games were at home to West Ham and Charlton, but we lost both and the knives were out for the manager. We were giving silly goals away and having to score at least two goals a game to win. We got our first point of the season away to Leicester and then had a resounding 5-1 win at home to Southampton and it looked like we had turned the corner. Two days later we outplayed Watford and gifted them a goal to lose 1-0, and we were back to square one. We were playing well but the results were not coming and the speculation about a new manager was increasing all the time.

Our results picked up over the next couple of months, but it all came to a head when we were well beaten, 4-1, at Southampton in the League Cup. Two days later Ron Atkinson and Mick Brown the manager and coach, were called in by the Chairman and told that they would be relieved of their duties, which was a nice way of telling them they had got the sack. I suppose to most people my reaction should have been one of gladness that the manager had gone but I felt the sackings reflected on the players themselves, because the results we got led to their dismissals.

The next day, Alex Ferguson arrived to take charge of the team and his initial task was to get the team away from the relegation zone. He had come to the club with the reputation of being a disciplinarian but I can't say that, in the time I was under him, I saw anything very different from Ron Atkinson, with the exception of the way the team played. He was more safety conscious. He did not believe in all out attack but he believed in having plenty of defenders back and restricting the full backs from getting forward too often. I found that I was in the team for his first four games and then I was substitute for then next three and then in for the next two. I felt that I could not get any consistency in my play because the team was never the same, it changed every week. Very gradually we started to creep away from the bottom but more often than not the manager would lose his temper and roar and scream until he went red in the face. At the start the players used to dread it but after a while it didn't have the slightest impact.

I was on a weekly contract and the manager had said that he wanted me to sign a new one, but I did not think there was much future considering that I was not being used often enough. I think everyone wanted the season to end because there had been no buzz about the place. We had lost at home in the Cup to Coventry City who eventually went on to win it, and we had climbed to safety in mid-table but come the end of the season there would be a lot of changes and I knew that I would be one of them. Nobody wants to leave a club of the stature of Manchester United but there comes a time when you know it is right.

I had kept in touch with Arnold Muhren since he had left two years before and I had told him that I would probably be leaving at the end of the season. About a week later he rang back and asked if I would be interested in joining Ajax, who were looking for a replacement for Marco Van Basten who was leaving at the end of the season. Their coach Johann Cruyff had always wanted an English style target man on his team and I thought it would suit my style since they played with two wingers. It was now up to me to get my release from United but it also depended on whether I could reach terms with Ajax over a contract. I got my release from United when my solicitor told Martin Edwards that if the club asked for a fee then the terms would be lower than what I was earning at United, so it was agreed that I would get a free transfer. It was to be a new beginning for me, having played for two of the biggest clubs in England, now I was going to play for one of the biggest in Europe. Just after my solicitor phoned me to tell me that he had negotiated a free transfer with United, the phone rang – it was Alex Ferguson. He said that he had decided to give me a free transfer and that the club could have asked for a fee of around £75,000. He was suggesting that he was doing me a favour and that he was making the decision when I knew otherwise.

My United career had come to an end and it was a real strain leaving a club that was renowned throughout the world. From the first day I arrived at United the media attention was twenty-four hours a day and the profile was very high. I don't think there is another club in Great Britain that gets the same media attention and it was a wrench to leave, but life goes on.

I knew it would not be easy settling down to a new language, culture and style of football but if the club helped me to settle in, I felt it would be only a matter of time before the adjustments could be made and I settled into their way of life. It was going to be harder for the family because they didn't have the day to day involvement of a job but they say the proof of the pudding is in the eating.

I can look back on my United career and say that I enjoyed most of my time there. I had a very good relationship with the supporters who never criticised me while I was there. It was a wonderful place to play football but only a certain calibre of player can cope with the pressure that is put on the players but I always feel at home when I return to watch games.

Me in Action

– 15 –
Dutch Nightmare 1987/88

Joining Ajax in July 1987 was, in my mind, the chance to start a new life and broaden my football horizons. It was a challenge and the chance to play European football again. The training was the hardest I have ever done at any club. For the first week we were taken to the north of Holland to a training camp. The routine was: early morning call at 7.30a.m., begin a pre-breakfast run at 7.45a.m., return at 8.45a.m., breakfast at 9.00a.m., depart at 10.15a.m. to the training area to begin training at 10.30a.m. Training would finish at 12.30p.m., lunch at 1p.m. and then rest for a couple of hours. Depart for a game at 4.30p.m. and return after the game at about 12.00 midnight. This routine continued for the whole week and, needless to say we were glad to get to bed every night.

I found all the players very friendly and helpful and they all spoke good English. I was living in a hotel, but was anxious to find a house as soon as possible. There was a general manager whose job was to look after these things and it was with him that I encountered my first problem. He seemed to think that it was up to me to find a house on my own, but I was training all day, every day and had little opportunity to get to see anywhere. In the end I went to see Johann Cruiff who understood the problems I was having and got appointments for me to see some places. It was not something I expected to happen because, when foreign players come to England I know that the clubs do everything they can to get the family and player settled as quickly as possible. I was not getting that response here.

Playing on the Continent is a lot different than playing in England. They prefer to build up slowly, transfer the ball across the pitch and play the ball when there is an opening. I know that this sort of soccer would not be acceptable to the English supporter who likes to see plenty of goalmouth action and shots at goal. It is very frustrating as a forward player because you can make half a dozen runs and never receive the ball, so I found myself increasingly frustrated by the slowness of the play. I was told to make a run to the near post every time the ball came across but more goals are scored from the back post position from crosses, than anywhere else. Because of my difficulty with adjusting to the style, I soon found myself out of the team.

We travelled away to Hamburg in a European game and went training the day before. We were doing some warm up exercises in pairs when one of the players turned me over and I landed on my back. I got up but felt a pain in my back all through the rest of the session. When I stopped and got on the coach to go back to the hotel, I could not move with the pain. It was three days before it was diagnosed as a damaged disc in my back, and I went into hospital to have the disc removed. I went through so much pain I thought I would never play again but after ten days I was allowed to go home. Johann Cruiff allowed me to come back to England to do my rehabilitation, something I was glad of because there was a lot of problems in the club between the board and Johann, and I wanted to be out of the way.

By the time I went back to the club three and a half months later the whole situation had changed. Johann Cruff had walked out after a row and one of the junior coaches was appointed as caretaker. As soon as I got back I knew that my days at the club were numbered. The most important thing for me was to get fit for the European Championship finals which were coming up in the summer. Out of the blue came an offer to play for Derby County on loan, but I had to prove match fitness first. The deal almost did not go through because the general manager demanded that Derby pay £2,500, for every game I played, to Ajax. It almost stopped the deal but in the end Derby agreed to pay and I was on my way to the English first division again.

I found the manager at Derby, Arthur Cox to be a straight guy who had a great passion for football and lived for it twenty-four hours a day. Derby were in the relegation zone and it was hoped I would help get them away from the bottom. They had England internationals in Shilton and Wright and a good blend of youth and experience, but their strength in reserve was poor and when two vital team members were injured they found it hard to win. I played ten games for Derby until the end of the season and I was grateful for the chance. I helped them stay up and and I had hoped I could make it permanent but Ajax's insistence on a transfer fee stopped that. By the time Ajax agreed to let me go, which was after the start of the season, I was without a club and finding it difficult to get one. I spoke to Newcastle but nothing came of it. Then I got a phone call from John Byrne who was playing for Le Harve in France, who asked me if I would go over and have a look and maybe sign for them.

I signed for Le Harve in October 1988 and only stayed until the end of the season because my family could not settle. The football was not great over there but the most difficult thing was the fact that we were not playing in front of big crowds. The atmosphere in most of the stadiums was non-existent and you could hear the players shouting in a lot of games. The French players were inventive but their game lacked the competitive edge that the English game had. Away from home the players just lost confidence and then it was back again in the next home game. When I returned to England I signed for Blackburn Rovers who had been in the play-offs the two previous season, so I was hoping it would be third time lucky.

I was asked to play on the right side of midfield which was a completely new position for me but I went along with it for the sake of the team. I found playing at second division level a lot different than playing in the first. Players tended to have less composure on the ball and the ball seemed to be in the air a lot. There never seemed to be time on the ball, the pace of the game was a lot faster but the quality was missing when it came to passing. We were in the top six most of the season, but the club was very restricted in its resources, not even having its own training ground. It amazed me how a club, who were one of the founder members of the Football League did not have their own training ground. We made the play-offs for the third season running, though I could not understand how we did it because we were very inconsistent in the final third of the season. There was a lack of discipline in the club and I blamed the manager, Don Mackay, who, to people on the outside is a disciplinarian – this could not be further from the truth. We were beaten in the play-offs by a very good Swindon team. The team needed rebuilding but there was no money available and players had been sold nearly every season to keep the club going.

It was no surprise, then that the team struggled the following season, since only one player was signed during the summer. We got off to a bad start and when injuries took their toll, the task became more difficult as the time went on. In the end we survived and I put my time at Blackburn Rovers as part of the learning process one must go through in football. I have had nineteen years in football and have enjoyed them immensely. I now have two boys, James and Scott and if they should ask my advice about taking up soccer as a career I would tell them to go for it.

It wasn't all a nightmare as is clear from this photograph

The European Championships:
Making Irish History

Belguim	**(Away)**	**Scotland**	**(Home)**
Scotland	**(Away)**	**Bulgaria**	**(Away)**
Belgium	**(Home)**	**Luxembourg**	**(Away)**
Luxembourg	**(Home)**	**Bulgaria**	**(Home)**

-16-
The European Championships 1986/88

BELGIUM (A)

When the squad for the first European Championship match against Belgium was announced, it caused controversy which was to last for two and a half years. David O' Leary was left out of the squad for the first time in a competitive international match. It made big headlines in Ireland, and all sorts of questions were levelled at Jack Charlton about the composition of the squad. His answer was that he had picked the best players available to him and as far as he was concerned that was the end of it. But the press in Ireland were not to let him forget it that easily.

The squad had contained four centre-backs, one of whom, Paul McGrath, would play in a central midfield role. As it happened Mick McCarthy had to pull out of the match with injury but no replacement was called up.

The match itself was the hardest we could have expected – a game against a team who were still buoyant after some wonderful performances in the World Cup in Mexico. They reached the last four and lost to Argentina, the eventual winners. Their side contained Jan Ceulemans, Enzo Scifo and the enigmatic goalkeeper Jean Marie Pfaff who, as it turned out, had a big bearing on the result. In the build up to the match we had been working a lot at playing the ball behind their defence. This had been the first opportunity for Jack to work with, what he felt was, his strongest squad. The next question on everyone's lips was whether Jack would play the three Liverpool players who had missed the end of season trip to Iceland.

Jack named the team after training on Tuesday and opted to only play Mark Lawrenson and leave Ronnie Whelan and Jim Beglin on the bench. I was asked to continue as Captain for the whole of the championship as there had been confusion when Jack first took over about who would lead the team.

There was a lot of tension in the stadium that night as it was the first time Heysel had been used since the disaster, some fifteen months earlier. There was a very large police presence which made it seem more like an Eastern European capital than Brussels. The game started off at a hectic pace and we went a goal down after fourteen minutes from a corner, of all things. We could hear Jack screaming at us to get the ball in behind their defence and not to play it square in midfield.

Well we got our reward with an equaliser four minutes later when I managed to head the ball past Pfaff, from a cross by Tony Galvin. From that point until half-time the Belgians were put out of their stride and couldn't cope with our long ball game. Nevertheless we went in 1-1 at half-time.

At the start of the second half they came at us with everything that you would expect from one of the top four teams in the world. We rode our luck on a couple of occasions, but were still giving as good as we got. Then, in the seventy-first minute they got a corner and the ball was floated to the edge of the box. There didn't seem much danger but Packie Bonner never got near Enzo Scifo's brilliant header from sixteen yards. We were up against it again, but from that time on, Belgium decided to sit on their lead. Their goalkeeper Pfaff was being very arrogant. Every time the ball was played back to him he would flick it up on his knees and chest and try to waste more time. With ten minutes to go, Jack decided to make a double substitution bringing on Whelan and Beglin for Houghton and Galvin. It turned out to be an inspirational move. With a minute to go on the clock Whelan and Beglin combined to send me racing clear of the defence and when Pfaff collided with me and brought me down, we had a penalty to save the game. Liam Brady was elected to take it and it must have been extra nerve-racking for him knowing that six years earlier, in the European Cup Winners Cup final in the same stadium, he had missed for Arsenal. I couldn't watch. There was no mistake – Liam sent Pfaff the wrong way and we had equalised with seconds to go. As we were going off the pitch the Belgian players were giving Pfaff a piece of their mind about the penalty. I thought to myself at the time that it couldn't have happened to a nicer fella!

There was great euphoria in the dressing room after the match. We felt we had done enough to earn the draw and it had given us a valuable away point. Jack said he was happy with the result, but not with our defending at the corners when we gave the two goals away. Our next game was against the Scots just over a month later at home, and the result that night guaranteed a full house.

SCOTLAND (H)

When the Scots came to Dublin, they came for only one result and that was a draw. They played with one forward, Mo Johnston and three central defenders with the two full backs not venturing outside their own half. The pitch did not help one little bit – the players boots were not visible when the players stood still. On one occasion Paul McStay tried a long-range shot and ended up taking such a big divot that the ball trickled about three yards from him. The pitch had been, for a long time, the subject of discontent and I couldn't understand why they could not have cut the grass down to a level acceptable to both Rugby and soccer. It was disappointing when one thinks that the I.R.F.U. got 15 per cent of the gross gate takings and they would not even cut the grass.

The match ended in a 0-0 draw and the press were scathing in their criticism as they felt it was a bad result. Jack, whilst obviously not happy with a draw, felt the lads could not have given more. Considering the conditions and the way Scotland had gone about their job, he still felt it was a good result. And, in the aftermatch press conference, he had said so. When some of the questions got a bit aggressive, Jack got up and walked out of the room. The frustration of the match had got to the press more that anyone else, but it is easy to criticise one event and then later, do a complete about turn without having to face the words that you printed months earlier.

SCOTLAND (A)

The return match against Scotland was in February 1987, and the press were again on the attack when Jack announced his team for the match. As he had a full squad to choose from, Jack felt he was going to play his best players in strange positions to accommodate everyone. His first moves were in the full back positions and he decided to play Paul McGrath and Ronnie Whelan in right and left back respectively. Mark Lawrenson was to play the anchor role in midfield with Liam Brady and Ray Houghton either side of him. The press thought that Jack had lost his marbles, as Ronnie Whelan had never played in that position and would be like a fish out of water. The positioning of Mark Lawrenson was accepted because he had played in a number of positions for Liverpool and besides, there was no one else to fill that role with the other positions already accounted for.

When the Scotland team was announced Jack said he was very happy with their line-up. They had picked a team of football players with two wide men, Pat Nevin and Davie Cooper. There were only three Scottish players of six foot or over and one of our strengths was the ability to stop people from playing.

We felt we had a psychological advantage as we went out onto the pitch because physically we were very intimidating, and we were going to make the match physical. After seven minutes we had the best start we could have hoped for. A ball from defence was played up to me and I was fouled by Maurice Johnson and Alan Hansen. As the ball ran loose John Aldridge put it down and put Mark Lawrenson through to score. After that, the Scots just could not cope with the physical pressure we were putting them under. Davie Cooper was getting nowhere against Paul McGrath and Ronnie Whelan looked a natural at left back. Jack's decision to play Paul at right back was further vindicated when Davie Cooper failed to show for the second half, replaced by Paul McStay.

The second half was very much like the first with their crowd, at times, getting very frustrated. While we still had not got that second goal, we defended ours well. Despite a couple of goal-line clearances in the last few minutes we kept our goal intact and deservedly won the match. The dressing room was a great place to be after the match, with the physiotherapist, Mick Byrne, leading the rendition of 'Flower of Scotland'. Everyone was delighted with both the performance and the result.

After the match the press had to swallow their pride and admit that Jack had done his homework on the Scotland team. The tactical changes had been inspiring and the press began to look at Jack and listen to him in a new way. He had proven them wrong and they had to be careful how they wrote their pieces in future in case they ended up with egg on their faces again.

BULGARIA (A)

The next match in the group was in the Levski Stadium Sofia, on 1st April and it was to be no April fool's joke. The first disappointment of the night was to find that the referee was Valente of Portugal, who had denied us a goal in a World Cup qualifier in Brussels in 1981. His refereeing had become inconsistent and he would give fouls for hard tackling. We had come to the match feeling very confident after our result in Glasgow. The preparation had been right, low key training and plenty of rest in between.

It had not stopped raining for two days and the conditions were very heavy, but it suited us fine and we set about getting a result with vigour. We were dominating the early exchanges and had put the Bulgarians completely out of their stride. The 38,000 crowd were not at all happy.

Then the unbelievable happened, the Bulgarians made a defensive clearance which was going towards our right back position. Mick McCarthy had got there first and was about to put the ball out when he was blatantly pushed in the back. The whistle never came, and as their forward ran free with the ball, he slipped it inside to Sedkov who scored from inside the box. Referee Valente had certainly been consistent with his decisions, they had all been against Ireland. The referee must have been the only person in the stadium who had not seen the push. We went in at half-time 1-0 down, and Jack was fuming about the handling by the referee and he told him so as we went in.

Jack's half-time talk was very calm and cool. He told everyone to forget about the goal and to just keep playing the same as we had before they scored. They could not cope with our game and sooner or later they were going to crack. The injustice of the goal seemed to make everyone more determined to get a result which was the reaction Jack had been looking for.

Mid-way through the second half, we got back into the game. Ronnie Whelan prodded a ball forward to me and as I turned I hit it in one movement. The keeper had no time to adjust his position and the ball was past him in the net before he knew it. We were back on level terms and the Bulgarians seemed to be looking at each other for inspiration. They knew that it was going to be a battle of character and they did not know where to find it. After that the shots were raining in on the Bulgarian goal with two being cleared off the line. Their goal keeper made two great saves from Aldridge and Whelan. Then with seven minutes to go the referee took centre stage again. As Sirokov, their centre forward went to take a ball, his legs were taken by Kevin Moran. Unbelievably the referee, some twenty yards away, pointed to the penalty spot. He had no signal from the linesman and Kevin said that it was outside the box when he made the tackle. What was more galling was the fact that Sirakov had been spitting at Kevin Moran and Mick McCarthy all the through the match and was now getting away with annoying the referee by diving into the box. There seemed to be no justice, especially when you had to play twelve men. The penalty was scored, but there was no time for us to get back into the game.

There were so many emotions in the dressing room after the game: the initial one was anger at having been cheated by dubious refereeing decisions, disappointment of having lost a game that we had dominated and a resolve that when Bulgaria came to Dublin that they would go home knowing that they had been in a football match. Jack patted us on the back and said that the spirit had been magnificent, that there was still a long way to go and anything could happen. We still had four games left in the group and the possibility of twelve points.

BELGIUM (H)

At the end of April we had to face Belgium at Landsdowne Road in what many saw as a make or break game for us in terms of qualifying. Their manager Guy Thys was a very experienced international manager and his team had got some of their best results away from home in the previous ten years. They would come with a very defensive line-up and hope to catch us on the break. They were also very clever at the off-side trap and had used it to great effect on many occasions before. Also they would not be caught out like the first game in Brussels.

They started with five defenders, four midfield players and one forward. Apart from the first ten minutes when Liam Brady had a good chance saved, we could not break them down and our crowd were very frustrated when they kept passing back to the keeper. The game petered out to a 0-0 draw and left us all, crowd included, feeling deflated. Guy Thys was very pleased with his point and defended his tactics as being right when coming to a place like Dublin. The press were very pessimistic after the game and criticised the players for not having the know-how to break down the Belgians. Jack disagreed with them and stubbornly refused to admit that it was all over for us, until it was mathematically impossible for us to qualify. We had dropped two points at home and not scored a goal, but there was still six points to play for and the hope of a minor miracle.

LUXEMBOURG (A)

Our best away game was in Luxembourg, the weakest team in the group. In our own eyes it was going to be a hard match but in the eyes of the press it was a foregone conclusion and it was only a matter of how many goals we would win by. This had been determined by the fact that Belgium had beaten Luxembourg by 6-0, and that we would run up a similar score. Being professional footballers we knew that we could take nothing for granted and would have to work for anything we got, and so it turned out. They made us fight for every ball and showed good technique and composure when in possession at the back and midfield, but when it came to the final third of the pitch their confidence evaporated and they were found wanting. We won the match with a toe-poke goal from Tony Galvin and a screaming shot from twenty-five yards by Ronnie Whelan, their first international goals.

At the start of the campaign Jack had said that he thought that eleven points would be enough to go through, and we were still on target for that with two home games to go. The press did not hold out much chance, but we felt there still was a lot to play for, even though teams were not far behind us in points and had games in hand.

LUXEMBOURG (H)

The return match with Luxembourg turned out to be a bit of an embarrassment. It was one of our off-days, when you hope you don't make too many mistakes and hope you get away with a result. The match itself did not create too much interest with only 18,000 turning up. The buildup by the press was low-key, as they had already written the team off as having no hope of qualifying. So the lack of interest from the public had contrived to make it one of our hardest games instead of one of our easiest.

After twenty-five minutes of the match we were making no headway and they almost caught us on the break on two occasions. Passes were going astray and it was turning out to be one of those days. Twenty-eight minutes gone and Luxembourg went 1-0 up, and against all odds they were looking capable of winning the match. But there was a bit more to this Irish team than a lot of people thought and we pulled a goal back before half-time when I headed in a cross from Ashley Grimes.

Going out in the second half we knew we would have to step up a gear if we were going to win the match. Late in the half, Paul McGrath duly obliged with a volleyed goal, but not before some nervous moments, particularly when they had a goal disallowed when it was 1-1. Late in the game Niall Quinn came on, so I moved out to the right side of midfield and Jack was shouting from the sideline for me to just sit and play the anchor role. He realised that it was safer to hold onto what we had rather than chase another goal, particularly when we were not playing our best. I think everyone was relieved when the final whistle went and the two points were in the bag. There is an old saying in football, that if you can win when you are playing badly, you have definitely got a chance when you are playing well. We were now top of the group with nine points. Bulgaria were one point behind, with three games, to our one left to play.

BULGARIA (H)

Two weeks after our win over Luxembourg, Bulgaria beat Belgium 2-0, to go to the top of the group. This result had given the match added significance and meant that we had to beat Bulgaria to stay in with a chance of getting through to the finals. For the Irish players there was no need for an extra edge to the game. This was one match each member of the squad had been looking forward to for six months. The two days before the match the lads were all bubbling with energy and in very high spirits. Jack was having to call a halt to the training sessions early because he was afraid of the players getting injured, such was the energy and enthusiasm present.

I think the press had realised how important the game was to the players and their buildup reports had been quite enthusiastic. This was the first time in all my years with the international team that going into the last match in a qualifying group we were still in with a chance.

From the very first whistle the Bulgarians were never to get a second on the ball. They tried to break up the game by continually back passing, but with the physical pressure being put on them their spirit was weakening by the minute. Liam Brady was having one of his best ever games for Ireland. He was going past two and three players with the drop of his shoulders and spraying the ball all over the field. Probably the most surprising thing for a lot of people was that Liam was winning a lot of tackles which was not a strength in his game. The Bulgarians had paid him compliment by putting a man to mark him, but it was not going to stop him, or the team for that matter, on this day. Liam had been booked in the first half for a mis-timed tackle and had to watch himself after that. The crowd were right behind us and the atmosphere was electric. Kevin Moran and Mick McCarthy were settling a few scores with their old friend, Sirakov, and it amazed me how he was able to walk off at the end. All this had been done within the laws of the game, of course!

We were playing the best football of the whole campaign. Ray Houghton, a danger on the right, Liam on the left, Paul McGrath just powering through tackles and setting up moves. The game was going on in the Bulgarian half. How we came in at half-time 0-0, I will never know but we were well pleased with the first half performance. For all our superiority we still had to turn it into goals and there was still the possibility of them getting one on the break.

We started the second half as the first, and the Bulgarians had started to scream every time they were tackled and were looking for a sympathy vote from the referee. But Mr Keizer from Holland was an experienced man, knew what they were trying to do and just kept the game flowing. We got the break-through midway through the half, when a long throw from Mick McCarthy was headed back out to him. He showed the trickery of a winger, beat his man and crossed the ball into the middle of the box. I challenged the keeper for the ball and as it ran loose Paul McGrath volleyed it into the roof of the net. The whole stadium erupted and the noise was unbelievable. Ten minutes from time we got another goal – Kevin Moran headed in from a corner after the keeper had misjudged the flight of the ball. At that point the Bulgarians just gave up any hope of salvaging anything from the match. But there was to be more drama before the final whistle. As Liam played a one-two, his marker body checked him. Liam struck an arm in retaliation and caught the player in the face. The referee had missed the first foul, but turned around just as Liam was striking his opponent. He had no alternative but to give Liam Brady the red card, as he had already been booked earlier.

As Liam went off everyone was on their feet and the applause was as you would expect for somebody who had scored the winning goal in a Cup final. The referee kept saying to me that he had to send him off and that there was nothing else he could have done. It was an amazing reaction from an official who had shown compassion, but had to stick to the letter of the law. The last few minutes were just played out with the Bulgarians not having the stomach for any more battles. We had avenged our defeat in Sofia and gone back to the top of the group, but the Bulgarians knew they only needed one point from a home game against Scotland the following month to reach the finals. With that in mind they were not too dismayed with losing in Dublin.

It was just under a month later that Scotland went to Bulgaria to play and realistically I thought the best result we could hope for was a draw. The Scots had beaten Belgium at home on the same day we beat Bulgaria and were playing their best football of the campaign, but it had to come too late to make an impression and it was a mountain to climb to win in Sofia. The day of the match I was in Manchester recovering from a back operation and not paying too much attention to the football on the television. England were playing Yugoslavia and winning very comfortably. I had called at a friends place on the way home and arrived indoors to catch the last few minutes of the match. Brian Moore was commentating that day and just before the final whistle in the England match he said Scotland had won 1-0 in Sofia. I did not think that I had heard him properly and when he said that Ireland had qualified I knew there was no mistake. After all the years of coming so close, that little piece of good fortune had finally come our way. I remember when I was at Manchester United, Ray Wilkins saying every time we had a goal disallowed or a bad refereeing decision, "It's all about qualifying". It does not matter how you get there as long as your name is there when it all begins. For the record Gary MacKay scored the winner for Scotland in Sofia which put us through. I think overall we had been the best team in the group and had shown that by only losing one match. Now we had the finals in West Germany in June to look forward to and with the backing of 12,000 fans we could upset a few more people and predictions.

– 17 –

The European Championship Finals 1988

When the draw was made we found ourselves in the same group as England, the U.S.S.R., and Holland and for everyone in Ireland the game that had to be won was the English one. It was obviously the biggest game as far as the players were concerned as well, because most of us earned our living playing in the English league. For warm up games Jack had arranged matches against Romania, Yugoslavia, Poland and Norway and it was after the last of these that Jack would name his full squad for Germany.

There were two things to shadow our run-up to the finals: one was the four match ban on Liam Brady which was later changed to three on appeal, and the second was the retirement, because of injury, of Mark Lawrenson. Here we had two world class players who were to be deprived of playing on the big stage which their talents justified so much. Despite that, there was still a lot of talent in the squad and as the time got closer the competition for places heated up. At the time of the first friendly match against Romania, I was just regaining my fitness after my back operation and felt quite rusty, even though we beat them – a very weak team – 2-0. The next game against Yugoslavia was a harder game and I felt a lot fitter and closer to my old form. We beat them 2-0 to continue our unbeaten streak at home to nine games. It was going to take a very good side to beat us with the spirit and growing confidence within the team. In the meantime Liam had a bad knee injury and was doubtful for the finals, though it was still possible for him to play if we reached the semi-final stage. I had a bit of a scare myself. I was playing in a testimonial match for Arthur Albiston, my old Manchester United team-mate when I stretched for the ball and felt a pain in my hamstring. My first reaction was that I had pulled it and having never had a similar injury I did not know what to expect. It was later diagnosed as a slight strain and meant that it would be very tight for a time. I rang Jack and told him what had happened. He said that I would have to prove my fitness by the 1st June, which was the date of our last friendly match against Norway. If I was not fit for that match I would not be included in the squad for Germany. It was nerve-racking stuff after that – I even missed my own testimonial match but with the help and encouragement of the Irish physio, Mick Byrne, who was always positive, I was convinced that I was going to make it

By the time the Norway match came round, I felt alright and played for seventy minutes with no ill-effects. Having proved my fitness, Jack went ahead with naming his squad for Germany. Unfortunately Liam had not made it and another player who had been involved in all the qualifying matches, David Langan was omitted and had not heard from Jack. David, who had actually played in four of the games and was on the bench for the rest, felt very hard done by. He felt the least he could have got was an explanation as to why, suddenly, he was not needed anymore. I think it was the biggest disappointment of David's career when he was not included in the squad. He had battled back after numerous operations on his back and knees and defied doctors who said he would never play again.

Jack had decided that we would have our preparations in Dublin and everything had gone very smoothly. There were outings arranged to break up the time between training sessions. One of these was a trip to the races which was an evening meeting and about a dozen of the players decided they would go. The meeting was at the

Phoenix Park and Jack came along to try his luck. Though not normally a betting man, Jack had a bet on every race, and every horse he had chosen won. In fact only about two of the players lost and everyone was in a good mood after the last race, so we decided to have a few drinks to celebrate and then make our way back to the hotel. When Jack was asked how much he had won, he said about twenty pounds, which meant he must have put fifty pence each way on each of his winners! Nevertheless, we all got on the coach and had a sing-song as we made our way back. Then one of the lads, John Aldridge, suggested to Jack that we should stop at the next pub and Jack said yes. It was all so laid-back, no one would have guessed that we were playing in the finals of the European Championships in less than two weeks. We had one drink and made our way back to the coach again. As we were approaching the hotel, the chant went up to stop at the pub down the road. Jack gave the nod and we went past the entrance to the hotel, had one more drink and left. The morale of the lads was high and if an outsider was to see this they would ask themselves how we had managed to get as far as we had. But these things were done at the right times and never affected the preparation or training we had to do. I just could not envisage England or Holland having a night out at the races as part of their preparation!

It was an early start on the morning we left for Stuttgart, a quick breakfast, suitcases on the team bus and one last photograph of the team outside the hotel. When we arrived at the airport there was a press reception, the last thing the players wanted (of course we knew nothing about it until we arrived), then onto the plane and on our way. I felt jet-lagged and we hadn't left Dublin yet! Two and a half hours later we touched down in Stuttgart and all the usual formalities were dispensed with – no passport control and our baggage loaded onto another bus (this was the way to travel!) – and then on to an airport lounge where there was another press conference. I suppose this was what we had to adjust to now that we were in the finals. It was something which the players came to terms with very well over the next couple of weeks. It took half an hour to reach our hotel and the first thing that hit us was the amount of police present around the hotel. Nobody was allowed into the hotel without being carefully vetted.

After a light lunch it was back to our normal routine – training, eating and sleeping. The training pitch was beside the hotel, so there was no security problems for the police and we just got on with doing our normal job. For the next four days this was to be our format, everything relaxed and easygoing, with no pressure. Liam Brady was with us, though he was working for ITV. It must have been really difficult for him having put all those years into the team, and now that we had finally made it he could not play. On the day before the match with England we went to the stadium to train. On the bus an armed policeman with a walkie-talkie kept in contact with a helicopter overhead. Now we knew what it was like to be a visiting member of State! When we arrived at the stadium, Jack told us what the team would be, and we began training at the same time as the match would start. It was very hot and we only trained for half an hour before returning to the hotel to rest before the evening meal. We watched the Denmark v Spain match from Group 1, and then it was back to bed for a good night's sleep.

IRELAND v ENGLAND

The day of the match the hotel was buzzing with people coming to collect tickets and generally to wish us good luck. We were told to stay out of the sun and to drink plenty of fluids. The reports were that there were 12,000 Irish supporters there for the match so we had to make their efforts worthwhile.

At the stadium there was a wonderful atmosphere. There was a lot of tension in the dressing room, but this was normal before any big game, each player going through his individual routine to prepare himself mentally for the match. Just before we got the call to go out Jack sat us all down and had his final word. What he said took the pressure off completely – he told us that we had done very well to get as far as we had, and no matter what the result was, as long as we gave 100 per cent effort we would all come off the pitch heroes. We all seemed physically relaxed and we went out on the pitch feeling ten feet tall. On the pitch we waved to our fans who were in very good humour, singing and enjoying the sunshine. For me, it was the highlight of my international career, leading my country out in the finals of a major tournament for the first time.

The game started off just like an English league game, one hundred miles an hour until some sort of pattern was found. It was another very hot day so energy had to be conserved. After six minutes we scored a goal – Kevin Moran played a free kick to the right hand corner of the box, I went for it with Wright and Stevens and the loose ball was put in the box by Tony Galvin. Kenny Sansom mistimed his clearance and it went up in the air, John Aldridge headed it down to Ray Houghton and his header beat Shilton and flew into the top corner. The Irish end of the ground erupted in contrast to the English end – just stony silence and no movement within the crowd. After that we just dug our heels in and put them out of their stride. They kept trying to play through their midfield and every time they got the ball they had only one option and that was to go backwards. We went in, still leading 1-0 at half-time, but knew they would have to try and change things to turn the game around.

At the start of the second half, it was apparent that England had changed their style of play. There was no more of the short passing game into midfield, the ball was being played from back to front for Lineker to try and get behind our defence. They were starting to get openings that were not there in the first half, Lineker had two chances and did not put them away. Peter Beardsley had the best chance of the match, a rebound from Bonner and ballooned it over from six yards out. We were certainly stretching our Irish luck by a bit here, and Bonner was having a blinding match. We were into the last two minutes and England had a free kick in our right back position. As the ball was played in, Lineker lost his marker and his header was going into the bottom right hand corner. Bonner dived full length to make a world class save. There was no way we were going to be beaten! The whistle went – that was it and we had come out on top against England for the first time since 1949! To say it was long overdue is an understatement.

Our crowd were going wild and would not leave the stadium until Jack came out to greet them. He obliged in due course after the television and press had had their interviews. He must have been the most unpopular Englishman in his own country at that moment. In the dressing room the lads all embraced each other but there were a few sore limbs! A few minutes later the door opened and a hoard of men in neat suits walked in and started to shake everyone's hand. It was the politicians from Dáil Eireann. This was an opportunity not to be missed – talk about jumping on the bandwagon! Liam Brady came in beaming from ear to ear. Seemingly, before the match Brian Clough had said that the two centre-backs in the Irish team were real weaknesses and Liam had replied that he would rather have ours than his. Regardless of what had happened during the match the result would stand for evermore.

After a night of wonderful celebration it was on to Hanover the next morning. All the English papers had slaughtered their team and one paper even had the gall to call us a team of mercenaries – no sour grapes here – not many!!! We had come from a team of no-hopers to having a real chance of getting to the semi-finals. Before the tournament all the experts(!) had said we would not even get a point and here we were with two!

Celebrating Houghton's fantastic goal

IRELAND v RUSSIA

Our next game was against the U.S.S.R. and our preparations were the same as always. When we arrived at our hotel we had a light lunch, bath, and sauna for the players involved in the game. Again, we were ordered to keep out of the sun. It had been a real problem in the game with dehydration setting in very quickly. Our next game was at night, so it was much cooler.

There was one change from the team that beat England. Paul McGrath had a knee injury and was replaced by Kevin Sheedy. It was a nice cool evening and it was like a home match, with no Russian supporters in the ground and ours who never stopped singing. The game started off at a slow pace and the Russians seemed content to keep possession in front of their goalkeeper. They seem to want to draw us in and catch us on the break, just as they had when they beat Holland in their first match, 1-0. When we got the ball there was no messing about, we took the game to them and were totally on top. They didn't want to know, and seemed to think that it was just going to happen for them. Not against this Irish team, it wasn't! It was all one way – surely, I thought, it was only a matter of time. Mick McCarthy launched a long throw, the centre-half and myself went for it and both of us missed it. In came Ronnie Whelan to volley a fantastic shot into the top corner of the net. It was the goal of the tournament so far. We were playing really well and they could do nothing about it and we went in, deservedly 1-0 up, at half-time.

Jack's half-time talk was about keeping the shape and playing to the same style as the first half. The second half continued as the first, except we seemed to be getting through easier. We were now playing the best football of any Irish side I have played with. Some lovely neat one-touch football and Tony Galvin put in a beautiful cross to John Aldridge, who was free at the far post. He elected to volley instead of heading and it went past the post. They were on the rack and we had to score again to kill the game. We had two more chances, both falling to Tony Galvin. The first one was saved, the second was caught by the keeper. With fifteen minutes left, a long ball found Belanov who mis-controlled, but the ball rolled to Protasov and he made no mistake. The game fizzled out and ended 1-1, but we looked on it as a point lost rather than a point gained. Some of the football played was terrific as it had come from the football brains of the players who saw situations and played the right ball using the ability in their make-up. Nobody can give you that. It is something you either have or don't have and we certainly showed that we had it that night! In the dressing room the players were devastated with the result. We had created enough chances to have won two games. After everyone settled down however, there was a deep sense of satisfaction that we had totally outplayed one of the best teams in the world.

Back at the hotel we were all having our meal and a few drinks to bring us all back down, so that we could get some sleep later. No one had seen Jack since we had arrived back at the hotel as he was still doing interviews with the press. We were all in good spirits when Jack came in and trailing behind was Eamon Dunphy, a journalist who had made venomous attacks on Liam Brady, myself and more recently on Mick McCarthy. I immediately got up and said that I did not have to sit in the same room as that 'shit'. Mick told Jack that he had made a big mistake by bringing him into the room and left himself. After a few minutes Dunphy left the room, mainly because he could feel the resentment his presence was causing.

When Mick and myself went back in, there was then a big discussion regarding the incident, which continued for about two hours. Jack said he had only brought Dunphy in because he wanted to have his dinner and could do the interview at the table. He said he had not realised the problems it would cause, but felt he could handle Eamon Dunphy. I don't think Jack convinced anybody that he could do that and totally misread how nasty Mr Dunphy could be.

But he was to learn soon enough and Jack was to become a subject of his criticism. He knew then why we had felt as we did.

IRELAND v HOLLAND

It was on to Gelsenkirchen for the final group game against Holland. They had beaten England 3-1, and needed to beat us to get to the semi-finals. The lads were full of confidence and everything was kept low-key, it was just a matter of resting and doing a minimum of training until the match. All the way through, our supporters had behaved impeccably and were a credit to the country. They had come to support their team and enjoy themselves in the old traditions of the game. The Dutch were a very formidable team with stars like Gullit and Van Basten. They would have the bulk of the support as the match was near the Dutch border, but our tails were up and a draw would be enough to put us through.

The match was again played under very hot conditions and it was affecting both sides. The Dutch started off well and penned us back, and we were restricting them to long-range shots but, we felt, with Packie Bonner in great form it would take something exceptional to beat him. We somehow managed to get a corner, and Jack had said that he thought this was a weakness in the Dutch game. The ball was played to the middle of the goal, and met by Paul McGrath and it crashed against the post. John Aldridge followed up but the ball was blocked on the line by a combination of the keeper and defender. The Dutch came back even stronger after that but we were working overtime to keep them out. Gullit was a handful at corners and it was the job of Mick McCarthy and myself to stop him, but he was such a big target to hit that we had to use all means, fair and foul to subdue him. The half-time whistle came as a welcome relief. We were all exhausted when we reached the dressing room. We hadn't played as well as in the previous two games, due to fatigue more than anything else. The lads had braced themselves for the second half and expected the Dutch to throw everything into attack but it never materialised. They were tired and their attacks did not have the same forcefulness as in the first half. The crowd were getting frustrated as time ticked away. The players were changing positions every few minutes and two forwards were thrown into the action to try and make a breakthrough. At this stage the neat interpassing had gone.

L. to R. Galvin, Ryikard, myself, Gullit and McCarthy

They were resorting to high balls into the box which was easy for our centre-halves. With seven minutes to go, a cross came in from the right and was headed clear. As the defence pushed, Koeman struck a shot which was going wide when one of the substitutes, Kieft, headed the ball towards the goal. This too was going wide. However, when it hit the ground it took an unbelievable spin and went into the net. It was a cruel way to go out after all the hard graft that had gone into the game. We were devastated at the end and it took a long while for everything to sink in. We had come so close, and changed a lot of people's opinions about the quality of player in our side. We had pushed the eventual winners all the way and at least now, everyone was aware of us and wouldn't under estimate us ever again.

It was an early start the next morning because we had to go to Dusseldorf to fly home. Most of the lads were in good humour though many had not had any sleep. We arrived at the airport and it was then that the lads decided to let their hair down. It had been a long hard season and it was time to relax. Keeping a person occupied in conversation while his duty-free ended up going for a walk or someone finding items of cutlery in his pockets when he was looking for change for a drink were some of the antics the players got up to.

We had been told that there would be a reception when we got back to Dublin but we were never prepared for what we saw when we arrived. There were people at every vantage point around the airport and thronged along the road all the way into the city centre. It was something I will never forget, for two reasons: firstly, it was my home town and to get a reception like that brought tears to my eyes. Secondly, the smiles and happiness on the faces of the people, young and old, had told us that we had brought a ray of sunshine into people's lives by our exploits in Germany.

Que Sera Sera:
We're Going to Italy

Northern Ireland	**(Away)**	**Spain**	**(Away)**
Hungary	**(Away)**	**Spain**	**(Home)**
Malta	**(Home)**	**Hungary**	**(Home)**
Northern Ireland	**(Home)**	**Malta**	**(Away)**

Training for the World Cup with Ronnie Whelan and Jack Charlton

– 18 –
The World Cup

The momentum from our European Championship campaign would, it was hoped, keep us going right through to the finals of the World Cup. Jack was now a national hero in Ireland, the people were behind him and he had the press where he wanted them. As long as the success continued the press were getting plenty of stories and criticism was kept to a couple of extreme cases who just reported badly for the sake of sensationalism and their own benefit. The group consisted of Spain, Hungary, N. Ireland, Malta and the Republic of Ireland. If qualification was to be achieved it was necessary for us to win our home matches and pick up points in Malta and N. Ireland.

N. IRELAND (A)

The first game was away in Belfast and Jack had kept the same squad as for the European Championship. It was always going to be a tense match because of the political situation in the country and none of our supporters were allocated tickets for security reasons. I was in the squad, but I did not expect to play. I had spent the last three months of the season playing for Derby County, but when the new season came I found myself in limbo. Derby could not agree on terms with my club Ajax, who had a new manager and he did not want me back. I was still under contract, with no team to play for. I had been training at Manchester City and had got myself fit, but I lacked match fitness.

The day before the game, Jack pulled me aside and asked what we were going to do. I said it was obvious that since I had not played a game so far that season he could not consider me for a place. It was a hard decision for me to make, but I knew it was the right one for everybody concerned.

As the game commenced we dominated the proceedings and had the bulk of possession. The game turned out to be like an English F.A. Cup tie, with people taking no risks and defending in numbers. After three minutes we thought we had scored as a glancing header by Tony Cascarino was touched onto the post by their keeper and had rolled along the line. Our players said it was over, but the referee said no. They only threatened our goal once when Gerry Peyton made a fine save from a Jimmy Quinn header. The game finally ended in a scoreless draw and again we felt it was a point lost rather than one gained. It was always tense and tight, but if Spain and Hungary were to get a result here we would regret the lost point.

SPAIN (A)

The next game was to be the supreme test in the group, away to Spain in Seville, a place where they had never lost a match. The squad had been weakened by injuries to Houghton, Whelan, McGrath and Sheedy. David O' Leary had been recalled to the squad for the first time in two and a half years. I was named on the substitutes bench as I was back playing again for the French club Le Harve. Jack had been forced to play Kevin Moran in midfield and an inexperienced Steve Staunton at left back. Regardless of that we knew that a draw would be a great result here. We were under pressure from the start and Packie Bonner had to make three brilliant saves to keep us in the game. In the dug-out Jack had stood up to get a better view of the game and ended up being pelted with fruit from the terraces. After the initial onslaught we settled down, but never really looked like scoring. We had frustrated the Spanish team but the supporters had kept behind their team. If the game had been played in Madrid or Barcelona, the team would have been greeted with abuse going in 0-0 at half-time.

Seven minutes into the second half the Spaniards got the breakthrough and after that it was one way traffic with Michel and Butregueno showing all their delightful skills. We had lost all shape, they were all over the park and only through good goalkeeping and last ditch tackling did we keep the score down to 2-0. The press had a field day and were criticising Jack for his selections. With the next game away to Hungary, they were sharpening their knives rather than their pencils! It was the first time I had seen Jack panic in a match, at one point he turned around and said to Liam Brady who was beside him on the bench, "What shall I do?" Liam advised him to put Liam O'Brien on and that's what he did. It was the first time in a qualifying match that we had been totally outplayed and it was a new experience for Jack to encounter.

HUNGARY (A)

The game against Hungary was a game we could not afford to lose. I could not even get on the bench and had not been told about it. The first I knew was when the kit man came around with the kit for the match and I received number seventeen. I don't think that is the way to treat anyone whom you might need on another occasion.

The match came at the right time for us as the Hungarians had just uncovered a bribes scandal in their league and a lot of their players were missing. We would never have a better opportunity of getting two away points. The game was there for the taking and we took control from the start. The Hungarians lacked confidence, showed neat skill in patches, but never really troubled us at the back. For all our possession, we only had an overhead kick by Paul

McGrath, brilliantly saved by the keeper to show for it. Jack urged the team to push on more into their box to try and get the goal we needed to win the match. It was not to be, they had two late efforts, one a long shot and the other saved by Packie Bonner with his legs when the ball came through a ruck of players. After the match Jack went on television and criticised the forwards for not scoring, something which was very unfair considering the amount of running they were asked to do away from the goal area. I feel it is the responsibility of all the players in the team to share the goals, particularly at international level. He singled out John Aldridge and Tony Cascarino as the main culprits. John retaliated in the papers two days later by saying that he had run his legs to stumps for the team and was tired out by the time he got into the goal area. I tend to agree with him because, if you ask people to take on extra work like defending in midfield, you are going to diminish their effectiveness in the box. With three games gone we had only two points and to look at the table it would seem our chance had gone. However, we had four games on the trot to come at home and those results would determine whether we made it to the World Cup final for the first time or not.

SPAIN (H)

The game against Spain was the big one. They had ten points from five games and were playing with great confidence. The day before the game as we were warming for training Jack asked me how I was feeling and I replied that I was okay. He said he was thinking of playing me but as I was playing for a second division team in France he did not know whether I was up to it. I replied that I did the same things in France as I did for the Irish team and besides, he knew what I could do and I did not need to convince him of that. I ended up in the starting line-up because John Aldridge was too distressed after the Hillsborough disaster. It was not the ideal way to get on the team, but it gave me the opportunity to prove a point.

From the first moment the Spanish team saw the pitch, they never stopped complaining until they got back to Spain. For us this was a great psychological advantage as they knew the game was going to be physical and were looking for excuses, even before a ball had been kicked. We were not to disappoint them and what unnerved them even more was the near 50,000 Irish crowd who never stopped singing for the whole afternoon. It was a wonderful feeling to play in front of a crowd like this and you could feel the tension in the stand before the kick-off.

From the kick-off it was non-stop pressure; as soon as a Spaniard had the ball there were two men on him and they found it difficult to get any pattern into their play. Ray Houghton beat Sanchis on the right and crossed low into the box. Ronnie Whelan went to the near post, but the pace of the ball beat him. It was coming to me and I knew that all I had to do was to keep it down and it would be a goal. Just before the ball reached me, Michel, their midfield player stuck out a leg and it deflected past the goalkeepeer for a goal. The place erupted amid scenes not witnessed before for a soccer match in Dublin, but there was still seventy-four minutes of the match to play. We kept up the pressure, and whenever there was any sign of us going below the standard we had set, the crowd would lift the team by encouraging and cheering. The Spaniards did not have the stomach for the fight and Michel and Butragueno were shadows of the players that had played so well in Seville. Only Sanchis had played up to the standard. I was substituted with just over twenty minutes to go, and the reception I got will be one I will always remember. Jack brought on Andy Townsend to protect our lead and reinforce midfield. I think all the doubts Jack had expressed before the game had now disappeared. The rest of the game was just as exciting. We were not to be denied and deservedly inflicted Spain's first defeat in the group.

After the game it was the usual ritual to go to the sponsors' lounge and have a drink with their guests, but the players had felt that we were being exploited by the sponsors and that they had failed to come up with a satisfactory arrangement in terms of money for the players. We told Jack after the game that we were not going to the sponsors' reception. He was not happy about it, but we just got on our bus and went straight back to the hotel. It was a decision that was taken by the players as a whole in order to make a point. I thought that that was the end of the matter until later in the hotel when I was confronted by Jack in a public area. He said that he was very annoyed about what had gone on and accused Liam Brady, David O'Leary and myself of having an influence on the team and that it had not been a decision taken by all the players. I told him that he was talking nonsense, that no one could influence a group of experienced players like that and that the vote had been unanimous. It was obvious that Jack had been drinking and he was at pains to point out that he had no individual contract with the sponsors, but had featured in all the sponsors' T.V. and press advertisements prior to, and after this incident. I thought that if Jack wanted to confront me he should have done it in private and he lacked tact by doing it in a public area in a very crowded hotel. As he was speaking to me, Ray Houghton came along and Jack then started on him. Everyone who was involved and in the hotel at the time, including his wife had tried to get him into the restaurant, but he was adamant. What was galling me was that Mick McCarthy was sitting in the restaurant with my wife and she suggested to him that, since he was captain he should go and try to do something about the situation. He said it was nothing to do with him and stayed where he was. I don't think I ever felt the same about Mick McCarthy after that.

On my way to an Irish record (two to go!)

MALTA (H)

The Spanish result had given everyone the lift that was needed. With three games at home and guaranteed full houses it was a matter of having our destiny in our own hands. The game against Malta was a foregone conclusion in many people's minds but the players knew that over-confidence could be the biggest undoing of any team. I retained my place for the game and it was one-way traffic from the start. The Maltese were content to waste time and continually knocked the ball back to the keeper. I had to go off after twenty-two minutes when a Maltese defender made no attempt to play the ball as I went for a header, and clattered into my knee. I was really disappointed because things had been going well and there were going to be chances created in this game. We scored our first goal when Tony Cascarino headed down a long pass to Ray Houghton who half-volleyed into the bottom corner. After that the Maltese, instead of coming out, brought more men back and attempted to keep the score down. It was not a spectacle but the result was more important than the performance. Ten minutes after half-time Kevin Moran headed in from a corner and the points were secure. We were to have more of a severe test a week later against Hungary, but with the crowd behind us and two points at stake to take us closer to Italy, everyone was confident of a good result.

HUNGARY (H)

Everything seemed to point to a win for Ireland in this game. Hungary still had their problems on and off the pitch, away games to come were to Spain and N. Ireland and, having dropped two vital points against Malta in two games, their confidence was very low. But football is not as black and white as that, they still had very talented players like Detari in their team and on the day could beat anybody. The game started off in the usual fashion with them pinned back in their half with shots by Cascarino, Aldridge and Houghton being saved or kicked off the line. After thirty-three minutes Kevin Sheedy got to the by-line, his cross was only half-cleared and Paul McGrath did the rest with a volley into the net. The score stayed the same until half-time. The only time they had threatened us was on the break but as long as we kept it tight we wouldn't have any problems.

The second half did not turn out as we had hoped. All the players looked tired; whether it was the long hard slog of the league season or the heat of the day, we took our foot off the pedal and it was the chance the Hungarians were looking for. Every attack was looking more and more menacing and their confidence was growing by the minute. In the seventy-fourth minute Detari touched a free kick to Garaba and his shot was destined for the bottom corner when Packie Bonner just got the slightest of touches. It hit the post and rebounded out. We were hanging on and the courage and resilience of the team carried us through. With four minutes left, Ray Houghton crossed a hopeful ball into the corner, the defender got there first but he fell over. Ray had a clear sight of goal and he crossed over to Tony Cascarino who headed it over the line. It was a piece of luck just when we needed it and it almost assured us of qualification. It was the end of a long hard season and the next game was a friendly against West Germany three months later. It was a time for celebration with the two weakest teams to play and the World Cup beckoning.

As our next game was a friendly one it was assumed that Jack would play as near as he could, the team that would face N. Ireland in the last home qualifying match a month later. But Jack, as unpredictable as ever, chose a team that contained a lot of experience – Liam Brady, Tony Galvin and myself were chosen when a lot of people had predicted a different team. The Germans, as ever, fielded a strong team, but were without their five Italian-based players. For my own position, I felt that if I played well I would have a good chance of playing against N. Ireland.

The game was going to be a hard one because the Germans are the most professional team in the world. They leave nothing to chance, their preparation and approach is first class and their techniques and attitudes remain the same throughout the ninety minutes. The game started with the Germans retaining possession, waiting for an opening before delivering the telling pass. For our part we were working well, making sure that they did not get in behind us. We had an early chance when Ronnie Whelan headed over the bar from eight yards. A few minutes later came a second chance. A free kick from Liam Brady was knocked down in the box by John Aldridge and after the ball had bounced around, a German defender tried to knock the ball back to his keeper. I had read his intentions and knocked the ball past the keeper before he could get on me. The goal meant I had equalised Don Givens goal scoring record for Ireland though it couldn't have been further from my mind at the time.

After that the Germans became more urgent in their play and we were chasing shadows for long periods. After thirty-three minutes, the equaliser came: the ball was worked from the right wing to the middle about twenty-five yards out and Dorfuer hit a shot which gave Packie Bonner no chance. A minute later the most controversial thing happened in the game. Liam Brady was being substituted and it was not yet half-time. Liam looked dejected as he walked off the pitch and only he can say how he felt at that moment. In my opinion it was a heartless thing to do. I wondered if it had been pre-meditated. Jack had stated publicly that Liam was not a ninety minute international player and this action was backing up what he had said. I felt Jack could have taken off a number of players. Liam was doing no worse than the rest of the midfield players and with the Germans' possession play we were all chasing the ball. They were making us work for the ball and upsetting our way of playing rather than the other way around.

Inevitably, at half-time there was an exchange of words between Liam and Jack. Liam felt he had been humiliated and that if Jack had wanted to take him off, he should have waited until half-time. Jack hit back by saying that his (Liam's) position was not more important than the teams. Whilst I felt that it was not one of Liam's best games, things were not as bad as they were made out to be. Firstly, we were playing a formidable team and secondly, we were not playing as well as usual on the day. It was a very insensitive thing of Jack and my mind went back to what he had said in the hotel after the Spanish match. Maybe he felt threatened in some way by Liam, David and myself, but he had no reason to feel that way.

We played better in the second half and did not give the Germans as much room and in fact, hit the woodwork near the end. It had been a good match, but all the headlines were about things that happened off the park. Later in the hotel, Liam announced his retirement from international football. I tried to persuade him to change his mind, but he felt too hurt about everything that had happened and said that if he hung on he would only be going as a spectator.

N. IRELAND (H)

When the N. Ireland game came along I felt I had done enough to keep my place. As I came off the pitch against W. Germany, Jack said, "Well done, you can still compete at this level". I had scored a goal and felt I was our most effective player on the day, but it did not matter – I only made the bench. I was right down in the dumps and I had not even been told of the fact that I would not be playing. It was a really important game and victory would assure us of qualification, but I did not get a word.

Billy Bingham's team were not going to be easy to beat and were causing all kinds of problems for us. We looked very tense and nervous and on two occasions they should have scored. The first time, Mick McCarthy kicked the ball off the line and the second, Packie Bonner had to make a last ditch dive at the forward's feet. Immediately, we went up the other end and scored. A long ball to the middle of the box was punched down and Ronnie Whelan stabbed the ball past bewildered defenders on the line.

It was a minute before half-time and we were leading 1-0, completely against the run of play. Jack settled the team down at half-time and the second half was a different story. All the confidence came back and two further goals by Tony Cascarino and Ray Houghton sealed the victory. The crowd were elated, but it could have been so much different. It would only be necessary for Spain to beat Hungary later that evening to assure us of making it. The game ended 2-2, but Hungary would have to win in Spain by five clear goals and we would have to lose in Malta for us not to qualify.

MALTA (A)

The match in Malta was really a foregone conclusion, if you can have one in soccer. There was a real carnival atmosphere about the island with 15,000 Irish fans there to see history being made. It was out of season for the Maltese, but the bars were drunk dry on the match day with not one iota of trouble. The team still had to have the normal routine before the match but the players knew that the hard work had been done. The game was nothing spectacular, but John Aldridge scored two goals to seal a comfortable win – **Ireland had qualified for the World Cup finals for the first time**!

By the time March came around a number of 'friendlies' had been arranged in preparation for the finals, the first of these against Wales in Dublin. Jack gave Bernie Slaven his first cap for Ireland. I was on the bench, yet again, and felt as if I was not really part of it. The game was really dour and Jack used all his substitutes except me. After that game I had decided that I was going to call it a day and retire from international football. I didn't know what I had done, but I could not be criticised for anything I did on the pitch. It was my wife who was the one who stopped me from making that decision. I did feel like an outsider for the first time in thirteen and a half years and that was entirely down to the manager. The manager felt he did not have to explain his actions, but I disagree. I was an experienced international player and deserved better treatment than that. But things were to get worse for the next international against Russia the following month.

On the day the squad was to be announced for the game against Russia the phone rang at my house. A journalist from Dublin asked, "Have you heard the news?", I replied "What news?" "You have been left out of the squad. Were you not told?" It was the first I had heard of it. On previous occasions when Jack had wanted to experiment with the team, he would tell certain players he was leaving them out.

For somebody who liked to be kept informed of everything that was going on, I felt that Jack was showing contempt for me. To be told of your exclusion from the squad by a journalist was the biggest slap in the face you could receive and the manager just shrugged it off by saying that he was giving others a run.

There was one more home match before the preparations for Italy began. It was against Finland in Liam Brady's testimonial, but I had to pull out because of club commitments. It had been nine months since I had played for the team and as Italy drew nearer, my chances were getting slimmer and slimmer. To be treated this way after nearly fourteen years was not right and with not even a word from the manager, made it worse.

The boot that broke the record!

– 19 –
The World Cup Finals
Italy 1990

The squad Jack chose for the World Cup was brought together in Dublin on the 22 May. The next day we were going to Turkey to play a friendly match and then on to Malta in preparation for the finals in Italy. When we were having our evening meal at the hotel Jack came out with a list of rules which he expected us to abide by:

1. We were not allowed to see our wives unless he gave us permission.
2. If we wanted to go for a walk, we were to get permission first.
3. We were also to be wary of the English press, who would be looking for stories, not necessarily about football.

To the majority of the players it was like being in school again and we were being treated like children. There had never been any problems with the players in Jack's time as manager, and our attitude had always been first class. We really could not believe what we were hearing! Jack also made a reference to the players' negotiations with the F.A.I. and the fact that the players had publicised what we had been offered. He said he did not like it and would not tolerate it again. The fact of the matter was that Jack insisted that we did not negotiate with the F.A.I. until we had qualified. He also said all the way through, that if the players had problems he would always come down on their side, but he had sat on the fence for months while everything was going on and then criticised the players for what they did. The people on the F.A.I. admitted afterwards that if we had not done what we did then, no agreement would have been reached. As far as we were concerned it was business, but there were no such problems when Jack was negotiating his own terms.

The game in Turkey was in Izmir on Sunday, it was 106°F at kick-off time, and it was going to be a hard slog. The Turks had just got a new manager, the former Danish boss Sepp Piontek, and were trying to get themselves together. It was a boring 0-0 draw, due more to the conditions than to anything else. I was on the bench again and was beginning to wonder if I had done the right thing coming. The atmosphere within the squad was nothing like the European Championships and this was because of Jack. He had been very short with everybody, and seemed to take the slightest joke as something against him and was certainly feeling the pressure. At that time Bobby Robson was being given a terrible time by the British media and Jack felt maybe they would turn their attention to him if England did not perform well.

We arrived in Malta the next day and Jack made one of the hardest decisions he has ever made in his life. He decided to leave Gary Waddock out of his squad and bring in Alan McLoughlin to replace him. It was devastating for Gary who had been with the squad all the time and I think that it would take him a long time to recover from this setback.

The training for the next week was very physical and everyone got on with it and gave it everything they had. The only problem was the hotel. It had not been open for business that year because of union problems and was only open for the summer because of the Pope's visit to the island. It was very run-down and was in the middle of nowhere. We were not there for a holiday but there was nothing to do when the training was done.

In the middle of our period in Malta there was an international friendly arranged against the local team. Jack decided to rest most of his regulars, but I still could not get a game and I sat on the bench again. Niall Quinn had given us a deserved lead and one or two changes were made at half-time. With thirty minutes to go, Jack told me to get warmed up and I went on for my 71st cap. Andy Townsend came on a few minutes later, and scored with almost his first touch of the ball. With ten minutes to go, John Sheridan made a great run from midfield, rounded the goalkeeper and crossed to me to score one of the easiest goals of my international career. I was to set a new record for international goals for Ireland. I had had thirty minutes of international football in ten months and it was to be my last game for Ireland.

It was another week before we went to Italy, so we trained and prepared all week to have a practice match on the day before we left. On the day of the game Jack brought in five of the Maltese players to play and left David O'Leary, John Sheridan, John Byrne, Bernie Slavin and myself on the side, watching. We had done all this training and he just left us to watch the proceedings without a word for any of us. We were hardly a happy bunch of players. The next morning it was off to Sardinia for us where England were waiting to try and avenge the defeat in 1988.

IRELAND v ENGLAND

The hotel in which we stayed was beautiful, set beside a lovely beach with trees all around. It was the ideal setting. The buildup to the England game was great, all the English press were asking if we would be able to repeat what we had done two years previously while others were hinting at a comfortable win for England. Those sort of predictions suited us just fine. It took the pressure off us and put it back on England's shoulders. The time for the match came and we left the hotel two hours before kick-off because the ground was fifty minutes away. We must have had thirty police escorting us to the match and a helicopter overhead. As we approached the stadium we could see the supporters making their way, cheering and having a good time. As soon as the game started the heavens opened and lightning flashed around the stadium. After twelve minutes England scored; Chris Waddle played a brilliant crossfield ball into the path of Gary Lineker and he scored at the second attempt, past Packie Bonner. Full credit to our players, they never let their heads drop, but there was not very much open play after the goal. It was like a typical English Cup tie on a wet and windy night. We went in 1-0 down at half-time but Jack told the lads to keep playing and something would happen. The equaliser duly arrived from the foot of Kevin Sheedy after he caught Steve McMahon in possession. The game ended all square with both teams happy with a point, it was important to get something out of the first game. Ireland had played the way everyone had expected them to and Jack did not apologise for that. England on the other hand had not played to the expectations of the press and were heavily criticised, particularly their manager, Bobby Robson. No matter what the England team did there was always journalists ready to have a go at the manager. I felt sorry for him. All the stick and abuse he had taken over the last two years were just not worth any job, but through it all the man kept his dignity and proved all his critics wrong at the end of the World Cup.

The Italian press had a field day, describing our match as the worst of the World Cup so far and the football as prehistoric. To be fair the match was no great spectacle but our style had got us where we were and the opinions of Italian journalists were not going to make us change that!

IRELAND v EGYPT

The next day we moved onto Palermo to prepare for the next match against Egypt. We arrived at the hotel and were not prepared for the shock we were about to receive. The hotel looked like a jail from the outside with little windows, without the bars. On entering our worst fears were confirmed. There was no air-conditioning and there was not enough room to hang our clothes. The food was very basic and the lads were far from happy. One player even joked that the IRA had come to blow up the hotel but when they saw it they thought it had already been done! The most galling thing about it was that Jack's assistant Maurice Setters had come out months before and actually picked this hotel.

The players, being the professionals they were, got on with the job in hand. Of all the games in the group this one against Egypt was the one we were expected to win. The Egyptians had played the Dutch off the pack in their first game, and were unlucky not to get both points but had to settle for one. It was not going to be an easy match as there was always the possibility of their quick forwards catching us on the break. The match turned out to be even worse than the England game, the Egyptians just played with nine players back and were content to frustrate us all afternoon. There had been a great atmosphere in the stadium before the match with both sets of supporters singing and joining in the Mexican wave. The match was a bore from start to finish as they had no intention of playing open football and set out for a point from the start. The onus was on us to prise open their defence and on the day we could not do it. Their defence coped very well with all the aerial bombardment and their centre-half particularly had a good game. We had only really one chance when Ray Houghton got through but their keeper smothered the shot before Ray could get it past him. It ended 0-0 and afterwards Jack was very critical of the Egyptian tactics, saying that they had come to spoil the game. All our supporters had gone home very disappointed, but would bounce back once the Holland game came round. On the day we had not been able to open up the Egyptian defence, what we lacked was Liam Brady but he was in the stands watching!

IRELAND v HOLLAND

Normally, the day after such a bad match is depressing, but our families were allowed to come and visit us. It took the pressure off the players and helped them to relax because the pressure most certainly would be on against Holland. It was the most crucial match of the World Cup because we had to get a result. The group was very tight with the four matches so far ending in draws, something had to happen or else it was down to drawing lots which would be a really cruel way of going out of the competition.

Jack decided that he was going to try a sweeper in training. It meant leaving out one of the wide midfield players, Kevin Sheedy or Ray Houghton. I thought Jack was panicking because he knew he needed to keep it tight. I said to Mick McCarthy that the defensive record as it stood was one of the best in the world and changing it would only bring more problems. Jack decided to try it in training and it was a disaster. The centre-halves were being dragged all over the place and our midfield players were getting into good forward positions too easily. At half-time Jack changed a few things, putting Niall Quinn up front instead of Tony Cascarino, because Tony had missed a few chances in the match. He switched Ray Houghton with Kevin Sheedy but still the gaps were appearing. In the end he decided to play with a flat back four, but Niall was to keep his place for the match. Tony was devastated. I felt he had been our best player against England, giving Terry Butcher a torrid time in the air. Now he was out of the team altogether, because of a couple of missed chances in training.

The Dutch had their problems too. There was talk of unrest in the camp with their manager Beenhakker, but this was always the way with the Dutch when the team had not got the desired results. I was speaking to some of the Dutch players I had played with at Ajax before the match and they were saying that a draw would be enough for both teams, preferably a score draw – but who was going to score first?

The game started with the Dutch playing well from the kick-off and forcing us back. They were playing as well as they could, all the old confidence was coming back and the passing and running off the ball was of the highest standard.

After twelve minutes Holland scored. Gullit played a one–two with Kieft and hit a low shot into Packie Bonner's right hand corner which gave him no chance. We were certainly up against it now, but the lads showed great character by playing good football and not panicking. We were taking the game to them now for they seemed content to sit on their lead. We had a John Aldridge goal disallowed and Niall Quinn was causing all sorts of problems with his height. We went in at half-time a goal down but we were playing our best football of the World Cup.

At the start of the second half, they tried to put the game out of our reach by getting a second goal. They had caught us on the break and Gullit had a chance to make it 2-0, but he hit his shot past the far post, a bit too close for comfort. Two minutes later we got the equaliser, a long kick by Bonner was volleyed back to Van Breukalen by Van Aerle, but the keeper could not hold the ball and Niall Quinn was on it in a flash and it was in the back of the net. There was green and white mixed in with orange all over the stadium but there was not one bit of trouble. It filtered through that England were leading Egypt by 1-0, and if the scores remained the same, we would all get through. So, for the remainder of the game, the ball just went as far as midfield and was then passed back. It was embarrassing because it was evident that both teams were happy to play out a draw. The referee called both captains together and ordered them to play proper football. The game ended in a draw and both teams were through to the last sixteen. The draw made a few minutes after the game put Holland against W. Germany and Ireland against Romania in Genoa. We had got the luck of the draw on this occasion and everyone felt we could make the quarter-finals. The spirit in the squad was the best it had ever been and the players had stuck together all the way along even after the bad result against Egypt. In our first World Cup finals ever, we had qualified for the next phase, a feat Scotland had failed to do in five attempts. From then on it was a knockout situation, so we only got one bite of the apple. It seemed like the whole of Ireland had been taken over by World Cup fever, something only expected in South American countries. We were getting clips back from Ireland of children in school all wearing green and white, also pictures of grannies dressing up in Irish colours whenever there was a match. I believe the publicans were not doing too bad either, the pubs were full two hours before kick-off time. Just like the European Championships, the whole country was behind us and people forgot their troubles and enjoyed the occasion as it happened. The players were aware of this and it gave us a much bigger sense of achievement knowing that all this was going on back home. Not even the state of the hotel could take the gloss off this result and the celebrations continued into the night.

IRELAND v ROMANIA

The game against the Romanians was going to be like a home match with our supporters taking all the tickets. It was an afternoon kick-off and this was against us as it had been in the match against Egypt. Such was the nature of our game that stifling heat was the last thing we wanted. There was a lot of tension in the dressing room and with the heat outside, it was very difficult to keep cool.

The Romanian team had proved themselves the best of the Eastern block and had a lot of talented players from Steava Bucharest who had won the European Cup in 1986. They had come through a group which had included Argentina and Russia and so would be firm favourites to get to the last eight.

They took the initiative from the start and pressed for an early goal, but we were defending well and restricting them to long-range efforts. Their best player, Hagi had made room for himself on a couple of occasions but failed to either pass at the right moment or get his shot on target. As we approached half-time there still had not been many chances and 0-0 was looking the most likely result the way things were going. The heat was sapping our strength and as the game wore on the pace dropped. Both teams were resigning themselves to extra time and then penalties.

Tony Cascarino who had come on for the injured John Aldridge almost broke the deadlock with a header but the keeper made a brilliant save. Just sitting watching the game was energy sapping, but the crowd never stopped singing and kept the lads going when it looked like they were dropping. It was nerve-wracking stuff – being a player on the line is even more frustrating because you know what the lads are going through but you can't do anything about it.

The extra time came and went and now it was down to penalties. Andy Townsend, Ray Houghton, Kevin Sheedy and Tony Cascarino all scored their penalties with ease and the Romanians scored their four and all was even. Their fifth penalty taker stepped up, looking relaxed. He took two steps back and strolled to take the kick, Packie Bonner guessed the right way and made a save – now we had a chance of going through. David O' Leary was our last penalty taker – he had never taken one before. He ran up and struck the ball home. In seconds the whole squad were on top of David and Packie. We were through to the quarter-finals of the World Cup. In the dressing room Mick Byrne the Physiotherapist was crying and going around kissing everyone – he had not done that since we beat England in Stuttgart. Everyone was so happy and there was a real togetherness about the situation. This had been evident throughout all of the games, a spirit that had carried us over many hurdles.

This time we went back to a five-star hotel, where they had laid on a magnificent buffet. A lot of the players' wives were there and Jack allowed the lads to have a night out. It was a night to enjoy and savour because no matter what happened from then on, we were heroes in the eyes of the people of Ireland.

Me with my wife Chris and sons James and Scott

– 20 –
Rome

The next day we flew to Rome and had a meeting with the hosts, Italy. When we arrived at the hotel it looked quite impressive but that opinion soon changed when we entered our rooms. There were two single beds in the room and they took up all the floor space, no air-conditioning and no place to put our clothes. Everyone was called downstairs by Jack and asked about their rooms, the same story applied for everyone. Jack then called the F.A.I. officials and told them that their rooms were needed for the players. They had been allocated the biggest rooms in the hotel, and they weren't very happy when they were told to vacate them. They didn't like the smaller rooms that were left, so checked out and booked into the plush Sheraton Hotel in Rome. When we got back to Dublin I was told that their bill for four days was £50,000.

Again the professionalism of the players came out and we got on with what we had to do. Our spirits were lifted when we were told that we were going to meet the Pope the following day. It was the highlight of the whole trip for every one of the players. Mick Byrne said that his prayers had been answered and was on the phone immediately to tell his wife Breda all about it. The visit to see the Pope made the trip for everyone – no matter what happened on the pitch this had to be the highlight. Just being so close and actually touching somebody you had wanted to meet for so long was uplifting in itself.

The stage was now set for our biggest test ever and things did not improve when we heard that the referee was to be Signor Valente from Portugal whose dealings in previous matches had been controversial as far as Ireland were concerned. I warned Jack before the match that if ever there was going to be a 'homer' this referee was the one. The day before the match we were taken for training at the stadium. It was certainly the best stadium I have ever seen. The Italians had spent millions of pounds to get it like this and to me it looked like money well spent. The surface was perfect but tomorrow night it would be a cauldron with the Italian supporters outnumbering the Irish in the stadium by far.

Before the match the lads were really relaxed, the most relaxed I have ever seen them in any match. The pressure was totally off them and on the Italians who had not only to win, but win with style to keep their fans and the media happy.

There was a fantastic atmosphere in the stadium, perfect conditions with no wind and a beautiful playing surface. They had so many stars on their team it was not surprising that they were the favourites to win the Cup, but it was all about what happened in the ninety minutes that really mattered.

The theme of Jack's team talk that night was one of accepting the decisions of the referee regardless of how blatantly wrong they were and giving a good account of ourselves regardless of the result. We started the game the better team, and were playing some neat intricate football, getting the blend right between the long and short ball game. We had the first real chance when Paul McGrath crossed into the middle for Niall Quinn to try to score, his header being well saved by Zengo. It was after this that the referee began to have an influence on things. Every time one of our players won the ball cleanly he would give a free kick to the Italians. Most of those were within twenty yards of the goal and very dangerous for us. All our free kicks were either in midfield or in our own back line. We couldn't get a pattern going because the referee pulled us up every time we got within sight of goal. The Italians got the breakthrough just before half-time, when Packie Bonner could only parry a tremendous Donadoni shot, and Schillaci sidefooted the ball into the far corner. He had been their star player in all the games so far and was top scorer in the tournament. It was the worst time to concede a goal but we had competed well with them and there was still half the game to go. The mood in the dressing room was one of anger. "The bastard is robbing us blind" or "I wonder what the referee's new Mercedes is like", being but a couple of the comments from around the room. It was all down to the disappointment of losing a goal and frustration with the referee's decisions. Jack told everyone to calm down that we were not going to get back in the game by being angry – we had to control it and channel it into our play.

The Italians were showing more confidence in the second half. They had a goal disallowed for a foul and Schillaci hit the bar with a tremendous free kick which Packie Bonner never saw. As the game went into the last twenty minutes the Italians closed up shop. They were masters at defending and holding onto a lead and we threw everything at them but it was not to be. We were out of the World Cup.

In the dressing room Jack Charlton shook everyone's hand and said he was proud of what we had achieved. Initially there was great disappointment but that cloud was lifted when it was realised that our country, with a population of three and a half million was in the top eight soccer teams in the world. These are the standards we had achieved and would have to be kept up if we were to maintain progress in world football. We had done ourselves proud and back in Ireland the public had taken us to their hearts. It was our first World Cup and we had gone further than anybody had expected. It would remain in Irish history for ever.

It had been nearly six weeks since we had started out for Turkey. We were going home again and to a civic reception which beat the one after the European Championships. The trip home was one to remember with the players' wives sharing the good times on the plane home. Before we landed the pilot took us over the city to show us the turnout of the people. All along the route from the airport to the city were thousands of people who had come to welcome us home and say 'well done' for our efforts. After all the dignitaries had their say at the airport, we went into the city, on an open-top bus, for a civic reception. It took us three hours to make a journey that would normally take twenty minutes.

The World Cup was over but for me it had never really started. If I had been told that I was not in with a hope of playing then maybe I would have taken the decision myself. Maybe Jack wanted me to take that decision by the way he treated me, by not giving me a run out after the West Germany game in September before the World Cup. It was very hard for me just to sit there after spending nearly fourteen years in the team. I had even got into trouble with my club, Manchester United, by evoking a clause in my contract to release me for international games, and began to doubt that it was worth all the hassle after being treated this way. I did feel very resentful, but I was happy for the other players and thought they deserved every minute of the success they got. I knew that after the World Cup it would be the end for me and the disappointment of not playing did overshadow a lot of the things that happened. It had always been an ambition of mine to play in the finals but it was not to be. It is probably the major regret of my whole football career.

Against the old enemy

In action for Ireland

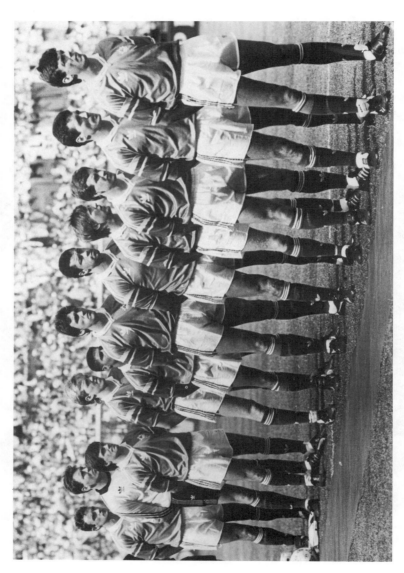

Proud to wear the Emerald Green

With my international team-mate John Byrne (next to me) playing for Le Havre

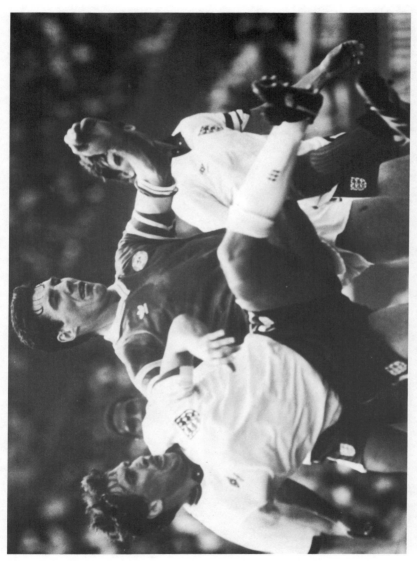

Getting the better of Kenny Sampson

Euro-Championship against Russia

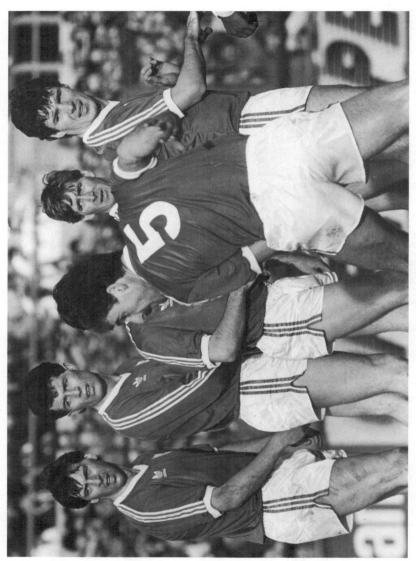

Where did it go?

Behave yourself Mick!

At one of my favourite grounds – Landsdowne Road

Sweating for the cause

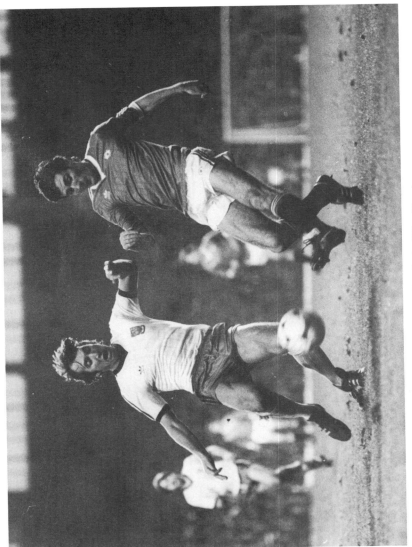

Beating Billy Bonds (v. West Ham)

Meeting the Taoiseach Charles J. Haughey

– 21 –
The International Managers (From Giles To Charlton)

1. JOHN GILES

John Giles's career as a player was one of success and when he took over as manager of the Republic of Ireland in 1973 there were very few people who doubted that he would also achieve success in that capacity. When John took over the job there were still many of the players he had played with remaining in the national team. He seemed to have no problem in stepping over from being a playing colleague to manager. It was his attitude to the job that began the transformation of the Irish team, from being a side that would achieve moral victories by losing 2-0, to a side that was looking to compete with, and beat the top international sides in the world. I was brought into the squad in the 1975/76 season, but I didn't get my first cap until the next season.

I feel, looking back on the situation now, that one of the biggest problems was the panel of players from which to choose. The main body of players that would be picked were from first division clubs, but if we got two or three injuries in vital areas then his choice was limited to third division or even League of Ireland players. So to compete with top countries, what was needed was to find more players that were playing in the first division. Of course, that is easier said than done. That option was exploited to very good success in later years but at that time the players were not available or couldn't be found.

During his time as manager John Giles brought a new professionalism to the job and demanded high standards, not only from the players but also from the F.A.I. Up to this point the F.A.I. had not really given the manager much backing, but Giles managed to get an improvement in certain things, though not as much as he was looking for. I think this was always a barrier for him in his efforts to do the job properly. There seemed to be more politics behind the scenes of the F.A.I. than you would probably see in the Dáil or in the House of Commons!

I felt I never really knew John Giles. Whenever the squad was together you hardly ever saw him, except at meal times or when we had to go training. He always seemed to be in bed asleep, but I suppose that had as much as anything to do with the fact that he played international football until he was thirty-nine. There was always a great spirit and passion about playing for Ireland, but I felt that something was lost in the period when training was finished and the players were allowed to go and spend the rest of the day with relatives. It became more difficult when players, who were born in England but qualified under the percentage rule, found themselves at a loose end in the afternoons.

Under Giles the results had improved. Playing in Dublin had been intimidating for every team but our away form had been very poor. When I went back to my club people used to say that they couldn't understand why we had never reached the final of a major tournament with the quality of player we had on the team. Nobody can really put their finger on the reason why we didn't get results away from home. Maybe the style we played when we were playing away was the reason.

Giles's style was to keep possession at the back and midfield and invite the other team to chase the ball, very similar in style to the

Leeds team that he had played for in the late sixties and early seventies. Away from home I felt it was asking for more pressure because, when teams play at home they naturally push on to you whereas away they would be a lot more defensive. I always found it very difficult playing on an Irish team at that time.

As a forward you expect not to get the ball on a lot of occasions when you make runs, but we seemed to hardly touch the ball and then spent most of our energy trying to gain possession back. There were very few chances created, especially away from home – coming off the pitch shattered and not touching the ball more than a dozen times.

I think John Giles gave Irish soccer a real sense of identification. He knew what was expected in terms of standards at international level and looked for that from both the players and the F.A.I. We never did achieve everyone's ambition of getting to the finals of a major tournament under John, but I don't think that his contribution should be underestimated on the basis of which he left. Stepping down in 1980 was a vital part of the success which was to come in later years. Things didn't happen overnight and it did take Ireland a long time to achieve this, but John Giles should be remembered for his part in it.

2. EOIN HAND

Eoin Hand took over from John Giles in 1980. The team had played one match in the preliminary round for the 1982 World Cup and won 3-2 away to Cyprus. Eoin was a popular player when he played for the Irish team because he would give it everything, even though he was limited as a footballer. When Eoin held his first team talk he said he didn't want to change things too much, but said he would like to give the front players a better service and more scoring opportunities. He didn't want the back four playing just for the sake of it but wanted them to play constructively. Eoin was a very approachable man and was always willing to listen to players' opinions and ideas. Some people look on this as a weakness but I don't, I see it as a strength to be able to communicate with people who work for you and be able to listen.

I felt that Eoin should have been stronger with the F.A.I. He allowed them to arrange a trip to South America and Trinidad without confirming the availability of players. I think the F.A.I. told him the trip was arranged and then told him that he had to find out what players were available. The trip was a disaster, with Ireland losing 7-0 to Brazil and then losing 2-1 to Trinidad and Tobago, a football nobody. After the Brazil defeat, Liam Brady said he was so ashamed that he couldn't go on and didn't travel with the rest of the party to Trinidad. Mick Martin stayed behind and eventually persuaded Liam to change his mind. If Eoin had put his foot down and demanded that the tour be cancelled then I think he would have avoided a lot of problems that surfaced later on during his time as manager. The good results that had been achieved under John Giles would be forgotten and these two recent defeats would be remembered until we beat somebody big again.

It was ironic that after that situation, the results picked up with great wins in Dublin over Holland, Cyprus and France. Eoin Hand came as close as any Irish manager had of getting to the finals of a major tournament. We lost out on goal difference to France to qualify, but still there was criticism from the media and it's there that I felt Eoin had failed. He could never come to terms with the criticism, particularly from one journalist who wrote his column with a dagger instead of a pen. I know that his family had suffered a lot of abuse and I don't think that any job is worth that. The fact that he was living in Ireland may have been a factor, but I believe you still have to rise above the criticism to maintain your dignity and do your job.

If the team had qualified for the 1982 World Cup we might have surprised a few people. We had beaten France 3-2 in Dublin in our last game and they had got through to the semi-finals of the World Cup. We had lost 1-0 to Belgium in Brussels after a goal was disallowed by referee Valente, who was to figure prominently in future games involving Ireland. We had two world class players in Brady and Lawrenson and most of the rest of the team were at their peak, but we didn't qualify and we had to hope that we could play as well in the next European Championships.

In the games for the 1984 European Championships we never reached the levels achieved the previous two years. Eoin had tried to blood new players during this period like Gary Waddock, Michael Robinson and Kevin O'Callaghan and for certain games it had worked, but we still were not getting results away from home and this had been the real problem with the team. Whenever we arrived back in Dublin after an away defeat the first thing Eoin would do was to buy the evening papers to see what they had said. By the end of the campaign the papers had started calling for the manager to be sacked.

Eoin Hand kept his job for the next World Cup. Even before the World Cup games began there was doom and gloom in the papers about the forthcoming campaign. We did not perform at all well scoring only five goals in eight matches and three of those came in one game. During the game against Norway in Dublin, the crowd actually changed allegiance and started cheering for Norway. By the time the last game came against Denmark in Dublin, our proud home record was well and truly shattered, losing 4-1. The manager's contract was not renewed.

For all that happened during Eoin's time as manager, I liked him as a man, but I don't think he had that toughness that is needed to be an international manager. I think he let outside influences affect him too much and in the end it got on top of him. For all that, he was just that thin line away from success and in the end he was probably relieved that he was no longer in the job.

3. JACK CHARLTON

When Jack Charlton took over the Irish team in February 1986, he was the first non-Irishman to take the job. He came with the reputation of being a no-nonsense man and with set ideas on how the game should be played, particularly at International level. At the time he took over the team it was the beginning of a new era for the F.A.I. They had just negotiated sponsorship for the first time and the money was to be spent in developing the game at all levels.

It is well recorded that Jack has not got the best memory for names and when we got together for his first game against Wales in Dublin, it was a 'laugh a minute'. He kept calling Paul McGrath 'John' and if he didn't know a certain players name he would just call him 'Mick'. Perhaps the funniest incident on the trip involved one of the lads who had been called up late because of withdrawals. His name was Pat Byrne and he played for a League of Ireland club. He went over to Jack in the foyer of the hotel and shook hands and said hello. Jack had been talking to Byrne for a few minutes when he asked if he was going to the game on Wednesday! When the rest of the players heard the story, they just fell about the place laughing.

But that is not the real side of Jack, he will give the impression that he is not quite sure of certain things, but is, a lot of the time, 'sizing up' individuals. He readily admits that he has not got the best memory for names, but when it comes to football he most certainly is very definite in his own opinion, to the point of ignoring other people's. This is all very well if you are dealing with very young players who you want to teach and drill your methods into, but with players who have played thousands of league games and have hundreds of caps between them, I think they expect to be treated a bit more like adults. Jack is very stubborn and likes to have his own way all the time, but I think if that was to happen it wouldn't be healthy. To have disagreements is fine as long as nothing is continued as soon as the disagreement is over. To be fair to Jack if you have an argument with him once it is finished it is over and there are no grudges held.

When we got together for the match against Wales, the first thing Jack was forceful about was the way we played. He didn't want it played about at the back and he didn't want the ball played square when we had possession in midfield. He said that he would rather give possession away near their corner flag than lose it in midfield and allow them to run at our back four with the ball. I suppose that's the defender coming out in him.

The Wales game was Jack's first and he did not have sufficient time to work with the players properly and get his thoughts across. Given that, we created enough chances to have won comfortably and ended up losing 1-0, the only defeat in Dublin under Jack to date. The next game was a month later against Uruguay the South American Champions, and in that game more of Jack's ideas were starting to come through and it ended in a 1-1 draw. We were never in any real trouble against a team who had come to intimidate in the best South American traditions. Still, there was not much time left to prepare for the European Championships which were set to begin in Belgium in September. There was a triangular tournament arranged for the end of May in Iceland with Czechoslovakia making up the group. It meant playing games three weeks after the season had finished and it was a test of people's commitment to play for Ireland. In Jack's eyes the results of games before the game in Belgium were not that important as what he wanted was a picture of the side he would play in in that first qualifying match. Of the squad that he chose initially (Liam Brady was unavailable because of club commitment in Italy) three Liverpool players, Mark Lawrenson, Ronnie Whelan and Jim Beglin went away with their club for an end of season break to Spain. This caused a lot of controversy because Kevin Moran, Paul McGrath and myself had just arrived back from an end of season tour to the Far East, also Ray Houghton, Dave Langan and John Aldridge had cut short a trip to Florida with their club, Oxford, to be back for the tournament. Jack Charlton openly criticised the players for not turning up and got into an argument with Kenny Dalglish over it. In the end Jack backed down and decided to forget the episode and said it would not be held against them. Not so for David O'Leary. When the original squad was announced David was not included and decided to book his holidays for the period concerned. When Jack found out at the last minute that he would be short of players he phoned David up and asked him to join the squad. David said that he had booked his holidays, everything had been arranged and that he had promised his family that they would go. Jack put the phone down – he was not happy. Now Jack had said on numerous occasions, that when he makes a decision on team matters that he doesn't tell the individual involved and that he doesn't need to. Well I disagree with that one hundred per cent. If, before he had named the squad for Ireland, he had sent David O'Leary a note or even telephoned him to say that he was not in the squad and that he would like him to be available in case of injuries, I am sure David would then have had ample time to make whatever arrangements he needed. But all David O'Leary got for that episode was a two and a half year exile from the National Team. I think there was another reason for leaving him out and that was because he wasn't Jack's sort of centre-back.

Jack likes his central defenders to push in tight on forwards and give them as little time as possible on the ball and this wasn't David's game at all. He liked to cover the centre-half who attacked the ball and use his pace to stop dangerous situations, so I felt the Iceland situation was a good excuse not to use him.

Jack's plans for the Iceland tournament in terms of personnel didn't quite work out but one of the strengths of Jack as a manager is that he can make the best of what he's got available, so we didn't have our strongest squad in Iceland. Nevertheless things went very well on the field even though there were not any journalists to report back to Ireland. There was not the interest, so they did not bother to come. We beat Iceland 2-1 in the first game and were quite happy with that, because in their previous two home games they had drawn with France and the U.S.S.R. We knew that the next game against Czechoslovakia would be a different kettle of fish. Jack saw the game as a chance for experimentation and made four changes before the game. They turned out to be very skilful and strong, but our long ball game and closing them down quickly really upset their rhythm. I came on as a substitute in the second half and scored our winner eight minutes from the end. Jack was very pleased with the outcome but he omitted three of those players for the next game in Belgium. They were Mick Robinson, Mick Kennedy and Pat Byrne – these lads were never to play for Ireland again.

To a lot of the media the trip had been a waste of time, but not to the players who had a great desire to play for Ireland no matter where it was. The benefits of the trip were not to be seen until we reached the European Championship games, but in Jack's eyes it had helped to get his ideas more into the players minds and the team into the way he wanted it to be. This way of playing had been Jack's idea totally and he said that he would hold his hands up if it did not work. Well, we had won our first ever trophy albeit a minor one, but it was certainly something to work on.

I feel bitter about the way I was treated even though I never thought I would because football has been good to me. To score against West Germany, the September before the World Cup finals, play well and then be just a passenger for the next nine months is too much to take considering the years I had put in for Ireland.

I always felt Jack had something about Liam Brady, Dave O'Leary and myself when you consider he tried to humiliate all three of us at one time or another. He had been the one who had brought up our names in a disagreement in the Airport hotel after the Spanish match. I also feel that the fact that I was on the players' committee, had been held against me.

Jack maintains that he will stay in the job as long as people want him, but I think he misjudged badly when he dealt with the Liam Brady situation after the West Germany game, as he did not think the public would come out on Liam's side and he had to backtrack and admit some of the things he had said were wrong.

A lot of people ask me if Jack Charlton is a hard man to work under. My answer to them is yes and no. He is alright when things are going his way and the team is playing well, but if things are going against him he looks for scapegoats and protects his own back. For example, after the Egypt match in the World Cup, he said that he could do no more than send the team out to play the match, but if they did not carry out his instructions then it was not his fault. Jack likes to think that he has got the press where he wants them but in the case of Eamonn Dunphy he cannot get anywhere. Eamonn criticised Jack for his insensitivity in dealing with the players and criticised his defence that it was done for the good of the team.

Jack has taken the Irish team to unprecedented heights in his time as manager and has got the whole country behind him and the team. Despite all that, he still has his critics, particularly in the media who say that the style of play of the team was similar to that of Wimbledon. Well, I don't think there is too much wrong with a team that plays in front of full houses at home against teams like Malta. What Jack has done is to create great interest in soccer throughout the country. To see the look on people's faces after the European and World Cups told the whole story. It can't be all bad if it makes people happy. I think the problems that come with success are ones every good team has to come to terms with, and that is maintaining the level it has already achieved. Regardless of what happens in the future Jack Charlton has already got his name etched in Irish soccer history.